design a
GARDEN
with
Tricia Guild

design a GARDEN *with* Tricia Guild

text by
Susanna Longley

special photography by
Michael Boys

illustrations by
Liz Pepperell

VIKING

AN ADRIAN MORRIS BOOK

VIKING

Published by the Penguin Group
27 Wrights Lane, London W8 5TZ, England
Viking Penguin Inc., 40 West 23rd Street, New York, New York 10010, USA
Penguin Books Australia Ltd, Ringwood, Victoria, Australia
Penguin Books Canada Ltd. 2801 John Street, Markham, Ontario, Canada L3R 1B4
Penguin Books (NZ) Ltd, 182–190 Wairau Road, Auckland 10, New Zealand

Penguin Books Ltd, Registered Offices: Harmondsworth, Middlesex, England

First published 1989

1 3 5 7 9 10 8 6 4 2

Copyright © Adrian Morris Publishing Ltd, 1989

Typeset by Pentacor Ltd, High Wycombe, Bucks
Colour separation by Bright Arts Ltd, Hong Kong
Printed in Hong Kong by L Rex Offset Printing Co Ltd

Edited by Anne Johnson

A CIP catalogue record for this book is available from the British Library

ISBN 0-670-82881-5

DESIGN A GARDEN
was conceived and produced by
ADRIAN MORRIS PUBLISHING LTD
115J Cleveland Street
London W1P 5PN

Contents

Introduction

D esigning a garden is a great challenge. Not only are there the usual design considerations of style and balance, but nature also has to be taken into account. Just as the climate, weather, site and soil conditions, seasons and plant growth are all in constant flux, so the design is constantly growing and developing, often throwing up some marvellous visual surprises.

Garden design is a partnership between designer and nature – and nature takes the biggest credit. That is not to say, however, that there is no such thing as a great garden designer – there is. One of the greatest of all was Vita Sackville-West, whose fantastic talent for embellishing nature with tremendous style can still be appreciated today at Sissinghurst Castle Garden.

It does, though, take many years of trial, error and felicitous accidents to discover some of the design opportunities offered by plants and gardens. So, where to start? How do you begin to cope if you have next to no knowledge of plants and a garden of lumpy clay and builders' rubble? We hope that, in this book, we shall give you some of the answers to these questions as well as inspiring you to discover more for yourself.

Planning a Garden

Whether you know a lot about plants or very little, it is useful when starting to plan to imagine that your garden is just another room in your house. Think of it as a space defined by its boundary walls, and the plants and features to be arranged within it as pieces of furniture, carpets and curtains. In this way you will avoid getting bogged down with complicated horticultural technicalities and you will find it easier to think in terms of what you actually want from your garden.

For example, what kind of atmosphere do you want to create: colourful and busy, or harmonious and restful? Do you want cosiness and privacy, or grandeur and an open view?

In this garden within a garden, through the dark and sombre archway a burst of colour evokes the sheer joy of summer. Twin borders of pink roses with tall mauve Verbena bonariensis *dotted among them and purple* Nepeta nervosa *at the front. The garden has an inviting, warm and carefree feeling. It is a style that is easy to live with and to maintain.

Views and Vistas

Left: *Hidcote is a garden full of views. A long central pathway creates a vista of an arbour at the bottom of this garden and also cuts through several different garden spaces, thus creating an interesting and varied garden walk.*

Below: *Tintinhull House has another great English garden, famous for its use of views and visual surprises. Always try to make a vista work in both directions – a visual full-stop at either end of the line of vision. Here, the round raised pond in the foreground and the gateway in the distance both provide focal points, so there is a vista whichever end of the path you stand.*

*I*f you're lucky enough to have a wonderful view of the world beyond your boundaries, then the layout of your garden should be directed towards this view: flower borders, trees, shrubs and other garden features should all be arranged to draw attention to the vista and not detract from it. If, on the other hand, you have no marvellous panorama, nor even a pretty glimpse of the outside to frame with carefully sited plants or an archway, then you can create a view within your garden using an eye-catching feature as a focal point – a dramatic-looking plant, a garden sculpture or a bench, perhaps.

Opposite: *this dark Yew archway, at Hidcote, provides a view of the garden from the windows of the house, but the opportunity to create a picture in the other direction has not been missed.*

Planting Patterns

Right: *this simple composition of plants blends and contrasts flower and foliage shapes, colours and textures in a gentle and undemanding sort of way. Tall, dark pink Centranthus dominates the bed from the back, while Artemisia balances the picture at the front. The transition between the two major elements is softened and blended by various plants of related colours, shapes and sizes.*

Above: *mass-planted ferns thrive in this damp situation. Their luminous acidic colour and dramatic, repeating shapes oppose the soft pastels and irregular shapes of the drift of Sweet Rocket (Hesperis matronalis). A mixture of large-leaved woodland foliage plants in the foreground provides yet another contrasting form.*

To help simplify the job of designing a planting scheme, you may find it easiest to start by thinking in terms of shapes rather than of actual plants. If you were furnishing a room, it would be like deciding that a tall thin shape is needed in one alcove, balanced by a low broad shape in the other. By building up patterns of groups of plants of contrasting and matching shapes, you can create a really eye-catching picture in your garden. Experiment by drawing up some different planting patterns: a repeating

block of triangular forms, for example; or perhaps a large flat expanse, backed by a dramatic vertical next to a billowing domeshape alternating with a sharp spiky mound.   To help you visualise how these could work, one useful idea is to take a photograph of your garden from an important viewing position, lay tracing paper over your picture and draw on your patterns. Once you are happy with an arrangement, then you can think about colours and textures to make your scheme more interesting.

Plant Shapes

Simplify the art of grouping plants by classifying them into a few very different shapes: tall flowering spires, like Delphiniums and Lupins; round-headed or daisy-like flowers, like Peonies or Sunflowers; dense, bushy shrubs like Azaleas or Hydrangeas; or open, arching ones like many of the shrub Roses. By categorising plants in this way, you can more easily create interesting and attractive planting patterns, since there is no need to think about particular plants.

Left: *the soft rounded form of the tree's canopy rises out of a dense cushion of daisy flowers – an effective idea that is also practical, since you can never mow satisfactorily around the base of a tree.*

Later on in the design process, you can refer to the Plant Catalogue (page 138), which groups plants into the main shapes that you need to consider and describes just a few especially good examples of each one.

Above: all the contrast is in the form of these two plants. Tall, neat spires are set against a relaxed, bushy-shaped shrub with round flowers. The identical colouring of the Lupin and the shrub Rose serves to highlight the dramatic difference in shape between these two plants.

Colour and Texture

Right: *one way of sharply opposing colours is to use a flower with its own built-in contrast and then echo the less dominant colour in another plant. Here, both colour and texture of the yellow Achillea match the daisy centres.*

Above: *this is a very effective complex of shapes, colours and textures. Creamy plumes of Aruncus stand behind the soft creamy spires of Verbascum. Sword-shaped Crocosmia foliage points upwards*

There are, of course, innumerable plant characteristics that should be borne in mind when composing a pleasing composition. Foliage and flower colours are obvious considerations which come next in importance after that of shape.

So much has been written and said about colour – the colour of leaves, flowers, fruits, and even stems and bark – yet it is so often underused, even by eminent garden designers. Gertrude Jeckyll and Vita Sackville-West are, of course, two of the most

successful and best-known exceptions. Indeed, it is Vita Sackville-West's use of colour-theme gardens that is largely responsible for our interest in and awareness of what it is possible to achieve with plant colours and their relationship to one another.

Texture also plays an important part, although it usually plays a supporting role to the main considerations of shape and colour; soft, woolly leaves set against smooth, glossy ones, for example; or light, feathery foliage set against stiff, spiky leaves.

Dividing Up the Space

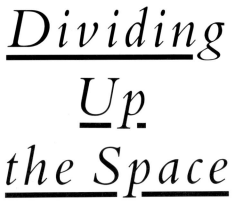

Once the outer boundaries of your garden have been defined, the space inside needs to be considered. No matter how small or large an area, its subdivision gives you the opportunity to adjust the shape of your garden by creating smaller and better-proportioned units. A long, thin garden, for example, is often far better divided into two or three linked areas than left as a whole, where it could feel like being in a bowling-alley.

Architectural Beech hedging and dry stone walling provide the interior sub-divisions here. The Rhododendron in the foreground echoes the Copper Beech behind from this viewpoint.

Hedges

*H*edges provide a solid but living structure for a garden, a framework which will give form to your planting as well as a plain backdrop against which your garden's plants and other features can happily be set. They can also lend a feeling of elegance and grandeur to the scene. Hedge colour, shape, size and style can all vary and your choice should be dictated by the type of garden space that you are trying to create.

Rates of growth differ too, so consider how much clipping time you're prepared to spend and how long you're prepared to wait for a fully mature hedge. Cost can be another significant factor – it's very foolish to stint on the quality and quantity of hedge plants.

Whatever the disadvantages, there is nothing like the clean and soothing lines, both horizontal and vertical, of a well-kept, formal hedge – its foliage dense and full of texture, looking from a distance like velvet, as in the case of Yew and Box.

Left: *look through this grand Yew archway to quaint Box topiary and Beech hedges beyond.*

Above: *an intriguing narrow vista is created here by chest-height hedges of Beech.*

Right: *this Beech hedge marks a change of mood, from formal beds and borders to informal plantings and wide expanses of grass.*

Miniature hedges, which range in size from about 4in (10cm) to 1½ft (0.45m) are for edging. They give definition to a bed, border or path and contain the planting, thus preventing it from spilling over. Box is a favourite plant for miniature hedging, although many small bushy plants will do a very effective job. Try double Chamomile, for example: it will make a simple 6in (15cm) high border and have pretty white flowers in summer.

Informal hedges are particularly in keeping in a country garden. Although they are clipped regularly, usually once a year, they are kept shaggy rather than being too precisely shaped – a

Above: *glossy green Holly hedges and topiary mark this garden entrance.*

little like a natural hedgerow. There are several flowering shrubs that are very effective when grown in this way: Fuchia, for example, or Cotoneaster, which has berries after its flowers. Mixed flowering hedges can look wonderful, especially if you choose the combination of hedgerow plants commonly found in your local countryside.

Right: *a low-growing Catmint hedge (*Nepeta faassenii*) lines this gravel pathway through the kitchen garden. It is perhaps intended to distract the cats away from the vegetables, since they find Catmint irresistible.*

Below: *Lavender* (Lavandula spica) *makes a similar but rather neater and slightly more formal edging to this front path.*

Hedges need plenty of space to grow – you should allow at least 2ft (0.6m) on either side for a clear root run and easy access for clipping. Buy hedging plants direct from a nursery: between autumn and spring for deciduous plants and in autumn or spring for evergreens. And always be sure to buy enough plants, since matching up hedging plants later can be quite difficult.

Generally speaking, you will need to space plants between 1–2ft (0.3–0.6m) apart,

depending on the species, and usually in a double row. You can, of course, buy quite mature hedging plants but, apart from the extra expense, larger plants may need staking and are much slower to establish. You will probably find, in any case, that younger plants catch up in size in two or three years, especially if you prepare the soil before planting and take care of your young hedge properly. Make sure you weed thoroughly, then dig and fertilise the ground before planting.

Annoying as it may seem, it is vital to cut back the young hedge by half its height in its first spring or at planting time. This will encourage dense bushy growth. If it is left unclipped, your hedge will always be gappy and bare at the bottom. Each subsequent year, prune away slightly smaller proportions of the growth made until the desired hedge height is reached. You can expect a slow-growing hedge treated in this way to increase in height by roughly 12in (30cm) each year.

Above: the formal structure of this garden within a garden is given by tall Yew hedging, shaped into arches over the garden's entrances. Low Box hedging contains the informal cottage garden planting, giving it a firm visual outline. The Box topiary of stylised birds, perched around the central axis of the garden, adds still more solidity to the framework – as well as a gentle touch of humour.

Drama and style are best captured by the neatly clipped, straight lines of formal hedging. These are the hedges of many classic English gardens, such as Hidcote or Sissinghurst Castle Garden.

The best formal hedges are made from slow-growing, small-leaved evergreens, such as Box and Yew. These give a smooth, uniform appearance, suitable for topiary and shaping, and need clipping only once or twice a year to keep their shape. Beech and Hornbeam, although deciduous, retain their dead, rusty-coloured leaves right through the winter; they are ideal for a very tall, strong, hedge that must also act as a windbreak.

All formal hedges should be clipped so that they are a little wider at the bottom. This maintains their uniform shape and encourages a dense, bushy growth. The heights of hedges should be thought about carefully, since they can entirely change the atmosphere of a garden. Hedges above eye level act like walls, making a garden feel enclosed and very private. A slightly lower hedge, from just below eye level to chest height, will still give a feeling of enclosure but also a hint of intrigue: it can't quite be seen over, but the plants on the other side peep out alluringly over the top.

A GARDEN OF HEDGES

This garden (below) *takes its inspiration from the garden photographed on the left. Well-clipped Yew surrounds the whole garden and low Box edges the planting areas; the hedges are much simpler, though, with only a little shaping. Central paths are wide enough to be paved areas for sitting out and the gazebo covered in climbers provides a focal point for the whole garden. The garden is an unashamedly summer one, and is a profusion of purple, blue, pink and white flowers. For balance and* unity, the opposite corner beds are planted in very similar fashion: top left and bottom right have white shrub Roses, Regale Lilies, pink Foxgloves and grey-spotted Pulmonarias; top right and bottom left contain blue and purple Delphiniums, blue perennial Salvias, Scabious, Blue Lupins, Agapanthus and tall Campanulas. Pots of white Regale Lilies stand to attention on either side of the benches, and Clematis alpina climbs over the framework of the gazebo, shading a central bowl of Violas.

Walls

A walled garden is many people's dream. The soft, muted colours of old brickwork or stone and the warmth and shelter they provide give these gardens a special sort of intimacy and privacy. There's something about the juxtaposition of the man-made with the natural that makes walls seem particularly appropriate in a garden – this is, after all, a place where nature and human effort are perfectly blended.

Walls make effective permanent garden boundary markers and are the best choice were space is limited. They can also play an important part in dividing up the internal space of a garden. And, as well as making a fine and instant setting for bed and border plants, they can support climbing and tumbling ones too.

Right: here, at Sissinghurst Castle Garden, a lovely old brick wall supports climbing Roses and Honeysuckles – neither of them allowed to cover the mellow brickwork completely. A Clematis, with its silky brown seedheads, tumbles over the lower walls on either side of the path.

Above: a climbing Hydrangea
(Hydrangea petiolaris) *is a very useful and beautiful summer-flowering climber which thrives on shady walls.*

Right: dry stone walls give you the opportunity to plant in the small crevices between the rocks. Here, Alyssum saxatile *has established itself and these are also excellent conditions for some bedding plants, such as Wallflowers and Antirrhinums.*

Opposite: the mixture of grey and beige tones in this flinty wall blends perfectly with the dappled effect of pale purple Wisteria.

A new wall is an instant space divider, whereas a hedge can take ten years to grow to its full height. Wooden or cane fencing is a much cheaper and instant alternative to a wall, but will need replacing from time to time and does not have the same feeling of architectural solidity.

On the negative side, walls – like hedges – affect the soil around them, drawing out moisture and often creating intensely dry conditions On balance, though, for principal boundaries, walls are the best choice, but remember to water and feed the plants growing near them regularly.

Above: *climbing plants are particularly valuable in a small garden as they take up relatively little ground space for the amount of flowers they produce. Here, Clematis × 'Jackmanii Superba' clambers over a lovely mellow and mottled brick wall, producing masses of rich, mauve flowers*

Beautiful walls should not be hidden by trellis to support your climbers and wall shrubs; instead use wires stretched taut between vine-eyes (wedge-shaped galvanised nails with a hole in the end for wire to pass through).

New walls can be very ugly, so consider rendering and painting them before putting up wires or trellis-work. Alternatively, you can age a new wall quite quickly by watering it with a solution of soil, liquid fertiliser and water – this will encourage mosses and algae to grow.

Because of the shelter they provide from wind and weather, and the warmth their fabric retains, a brick or stone wall offers tremendous scope for growing climbing plants and wall-trained shrubs and trees.

In frost-prone areas, a high garden wall is the best spot against which to grow fruits, such as apricots, peaches and nectarines. In early spring you can hook some polythene sheeting to the wall and drape it down over your plants to protect the blossom from frost.

A WALLED GARDEN

This small town garden (below) is fortunate enough to be bounded on all sides by brick walls. Maximum use has been made of these to support climbing plants, such as the white climbing Rose, yellow variegated Ivy, yellow bell-flowered Clematis tangutica, climbing Hydrangea and Wisteria.

To make the area feel more open and spacious as well as drawing attention to the boundary walls, the design has been kept uncluttered, leaving a wide uninterrupted central expanse. The space is broken up horizontally by the change in levels and the use of different ground surfacing in the two areas so created.

The two large trees (both Robinia pseudoacacia 'Frisia') give a little shade and some extra privacy, as well as providing focal points to draw the eye. The deep bed on the right helps to link the two areas, being both on a level with, and therefore part of, the upper lawned area as well as a raised bed for the lower garden. This feature also balances the paved expanse. The space is broken sitting area at the end of the plot. Bold-leaved plants dominate the planting scheme: Bergenia cordifolia (bottom left-hand corner), the Arum Lily Zantedeschia aethiopica 'Crowborough' with its spear-shaped leaves, and Euphorbia characias next to it. Opposite, in the raised bed, large clumps of bamboo arch over the yellow Day Lilies and Iris, which have tiny white-flowered Violas creeping among them.

Archways and Pergolas

*T*hese structures help to create atmosphere; you really feel 'inside' a garden – almost part of it – as you wander under a plant-clad arch through into the view beyond. Those who want to create a beautiful garden in six months rather than two years would do well to incorporate an archway or pergola in their plan, since they seem to give an almost instant feeling of maturity.

As far as the plants are concerned, suitable climbers abound. In fact, most will relish the airy atmosphere provided by an archway as opposed to the often too hot and humid conditions provided by a wall or fence. For example, many climbing and rambling roses invariably fall prey to mildew and other fungal infections when grown close to a solid support. Archways or pergolas are ideal for them since their stems are kept well ventilated.

Left: *a galvanised iron framework, densely clothed with climbing Roses, helps to dramatise this spectacular sight. The darkness under the archway contrasts vividly with the colourful scene beyond.*

Above: *surrounded by flowers in the White Garden at Sissinghurst, the central pergola is covered in the white blossom of* Rosa filipes *'Kiftsgate'.*

Right: *white Jasmine scrambles up this small archway and wafts its gorgeous scent over anyone lucky enough to pass beneath it.*

As well as framing the view and giving instant height to a planted area, archways can have a very pleasing effect in those passing or sitting beneath them: the awareness of an overhead structure makes the area feel very secure and private, and yet with a privileged view or vantage point.

Archways and pergolas make the perfect supports for scented climbers, especially those that like plenty of air circulating around them – such as many of the beautiful but mildew-prone Roses, like *Rosa* 'Mme Gregoire Staechelin', *R.* 'Zephirine Drouhin' or *R.* 'Albertine'. In the shelter of an archway at flowering time, the still air traps the perfume so you can sample it as you wander through.

Above: *this tall, dark archway of Yew, reinforced by the upright conifers on either side of the steps, frames the view of the blue bench on the raised walkway. Without the bench, the archway would seem a little pointless.*

Above: a living archway can be created by the branches of closely planted avenues of trees. Shown here is the 'Nuttery' at Sissinghurst Castle Garden: the nut trees form a series of arches, not for walking under but to provide a vista through to the statues and then on to the countryside beyond.

A pergola, or a series of linked archways, is a particularly good idea for a town garden – where views and sounds need to be excluded not only from the neighbours on either side but often from people in the flats above too. Sound travels alarmingly efficiently where there are a lot of buildings off which it can reverberate, and a leafy screen of luxuriant vegetation is very good at reducing its effect.

Archways and pergolas can either be built on site, with brick or timber uprights and timber crosspieces, or you can buy them ready-made in metal or timber. If you are lucky, you can sometimes buy old ones from architectural salvage companies

A GARDEN OF ARCHES

This silver and pink garden (below) takes archways as its central design theme. The garden moves from the relative formality and neatness of the paved area just outside the house, with its metal framed arches clothed in Wisteria, to a roughly mown orchard where the canopies of apple trees form the archway.

These two gardens are divided by a small flowerbed, backed by a low wall covered in Clematis, running across the plot. The gardens are linked, both thematically and visually, by the archways and the gravel path which form a continuous vista from the back door to the summer house at the end of the garden.

Garden Themes

*W*hen designing anything at all – whether a teapot or a house – it helps to have a theme to follow. This will provide you with a constant link that can guide all your decision making.

Garden themes can be about anything you like. Colour is a favourite one – a blue garden, for example, or a white one; a particular style can be another, such as a cottage garden or a Victorian garden.

To be really helpful, a design theme must be very well defined. Without this clarity of thought, the design 'message' may simply fail to come across. In the following pages, possible interpretations of several themes are given – and we hope that these will inspire you to choose one of your own.

Contrasting foliage forms could be said to be the main theme in this scheme, with its planting in large natural-looking drifts.

The Country Garden

A cottage garden with a little more style is how you could describe the Country Garden. These are not just flowers dotted everywhere in a formless, haphazard muddle, but large intentional shows of colour and form that hang together in a strong overall layout. It is a theme perhaps best suited to a house in the country, but there's no reason at all why it shouldn't be used elsewhere – even in the city – although a good-sized garden would be necessary to transmit a feeling of relaxed extensiveness, unrestricted by garden boundaries.

Left: *a consciously thought-out plan, not a cottage garden jumble, has given rise to this yellow, orange and red Country Flower Garden. Flowers include yellow Day-lilies, orange Wallflowers, red and yellow Aquilegias, red Poppies, the yellow-flowered climber* Fremontia californica, *and many others.*

Right: *from this point of view, you can more fully appreciate the extensive and informal feeling of the same Country Garden shown on the previous page. The generous clumps of plants and the gently undulating ground become increasingly relaxed and countryfied as you move away from the house.*

Left: *this weathered copper container provides a round central feature in a round paved area, where yellow and red flowers predominate. The metal pot also makes a bold full-stop to the straight path, leading from the contrasting country garden beyond.*

As your garden design plan progresses, the need for a design theme becomes increasingly imperative, since it can help you decide what kind of path or pergola is called for or what sort of fencing to use. An area of land will often, by its location or by existing permanent features, suggest a theme. A country theme is often very suitable for an oddly shaped piece of ground since, in this situation, regular shapes are inappropriate.

Rustic post-and-rail fences, dry-stone walls, white pailings, wooden benches, a large informal pond, and crushed bark pathways are all suitable for the country garden, but don't get too bogged down with getting the details 'right'.

Above all, the area should not appear 'over-designed' and perfect, but should have a relaxed and easy-going feel. In other words there is no need to follow your principal design theme too obsessively. This may seem contradictory, but it's appropriate here to allow nature plenty of scope.

Opposite: *a beautiful and varied combination of colours and textures. Strong dark pink Peonies provide a solid background, while the palest purple, fluffy Nigella and lime-green Euphorbia fill the gap behind the dramatic Iris foliage, which disguises the rather tatty leaves of the mauve Ornamental Onion.*

Above: *a homely and informal effect is shown here, using some traditional cottage garden plants such as Poppies, Sweet Rocket, Foxgloves, and Honesty.*

Always start the practical side of planning by doing a rough scale drawing of your house and garden, locating the position of any immovables, such as mature trees, front door, garage, and so on. Then, using tracing paper overlays on top of your sketch, you can experiment with different layouts. This process should help you to develop your garden 'theme' if you haven't already chosen one.

The Country Garden layout can be as symmetrical or as asymmetrical as you like, since the plants will soften the rigidity of any straight lines. Do bear in mind, however, that non-uniform curving flowerbeds rarely work well mixed with symmetrical borders.

For the main layout of access paths and so on, it's usually best to follow any lines leading from the doors of the house. If you decide on meandering paths – which would be perfectly appropriate in a country garden – make sure that the meanders exist for a purpose: plant a tree or a large shrub, for example, or place a rock or some other object in the line of the path – the bend will then look completely natural.

It is a good idea to consider certain practicalities at an early stage in planning. Where are you going to put the garden rubbish? Where is the best place for sitting? Are there any views that need to be obscured? You can then allow for these and incorporate them into your layout.

Garden buildings, such as sheds, garages and pavilions, should always reflect the style of your garden. Remember that a building will attract the eye even if it has not been designed as a focal point. In a country garden, where you are trying to create an easy-going, informal feeling, you can be as fanciful as you like – although a rustic or a period style would be more suitable than a modern one; the idea of a rather grand, but tiny, classical folly peering out from an unkempt jungle of flowers, trees and shrubs is certainly appealing.

Whatever style you choose, instead of buying a building 'off the peg' or having a conventional one built, take a look around a few junk yards, antique shops and auction rooms for a characterful chunk of architecture – a window frame or a beautiful door or even a piece of stonework – then design your building around it. If you've been lumbered with a hideous-looking building, try re-roofing it with old pantiles and white-washing the walls.

THE COUNTRY GARDEN

In this garden plan (below) the theme of the country garden is repeated and extended. The unmanicured lawn is good for garden games and picnics in fine weather, and the traditional teak bench in the shade of a small tree is an ideal place for communing with nature.

Old-fashioned cottage-garden plants dominate the planting scheme. At the bottom left, a clump of plain green Hostas grow in front of a pale pink Peony. Tiarella, with fluffy white flowers, covers the ground in the bottom left corner, and Honeysuckle clambers over the adjacent wall. In the left hand border, pink, salmon and dark crimson shrub Roses are intermingled with dark pink

Peonies. The theme of pinkish flowerheads is continued with the large purple-mauve pompons of Onion flowers, the pinky white froth of London Pride, and the small purple clusters of Tradescantia blooms nestling among its leaves.

The bed edging the path is largely devoted to different Iris varieties. Among them grow Euphorbia, Nigella and more Onion flowers, and the bed is edged with a golden mossy Saxifrage. Clumps of yellow Day-lilies are backed by a pink climbing Rose in the top left-hand corner of the garden. Along the far bed, Catmint spills over old-fashioned bed-edging along the far bed, alongside crimson Peonies and white

Day-lilies. On the right-hand side, Tiarella and London Pride reappear but this time with pink Poppies and more Catmint. Honeysuckle and orange-flowered Nasturtiums scramble over the ground and up the right-hand wall.

The large tree is an apple and the smaller one, beside the bench, a crab apple to provide the other tree with pollen. The right-hand bottom corner is given over mainly to white and yellow flowers – in the foreground yellow Iris and Day-lilies, Anthemis daisies, dwarf Achillea and Japanese Anemones are backed by a bush of Choisya, the Mexican Orange, a white Peony, a clump of lime-green Euphorbia and a red-berried Skimmia bush.

The Shady Garden

You can use the natural conditions and constraints of your garden to give you a design theme. Every garden has a shaded area – caused either by buildings or large plants growing nearby. Shade makes a good garden theme, since there are several common and visible characters of colour and form that tend to go with shade tolerance, and plants with these characters will obviously look more appropriate here.

With shade comes coolness, and many characteristics follow from that. Take colour, for example. Cool greens, blues, mauves and whites usually look more at home in the shade than warm colours like bright orange, reds and yellows. Soft, woolly grey foliage somehow goes with warm, dry, sunny places, so this is best avoided if your design theme is shade.

Coolness also goes with dampness and leafiness. Large leaves are a common characteristic of moisture-loving shade plants, the foliage being designed to collect as much light as possible. There are plenty of these plants to choose from.

Left: *in this damp area of dappled shade, the large-leaved* Gunnera *will soon grow to tower over the bluish rounded* Hosta sieboldiana: *pink and mauve Candelabra Primulas add a touch of colour to the cool, leafy scene.*

Above: *these magical little yellow Poppies (*Meconopsis cambrica*) will seed themselves until they completely smother the ground. They'll grow in sun or shade, but to do well in the shade they must have a well-drained, sandy soil.*

Left: *Lily-ot-the-valley (*Convallaria majalis*) is a very easy-going plant that does not mind what kind of soil it has – clay, sand, chalky or peaty – and it'll spread over the ground, colonising even quite shaded areas.*

Opposite: *lush green feathery fern fronds and large glossy-leaved* Lysichiton americanus *thrive in the shade of trees and shrubs, where the soil is permanently damp.*

Dry shade, the conditions often found at the foot of a shaded wall or hedge, can be a little more limiting in terms of the range of plants available. The Epimediums are particularly tolerant of these conditions and will make pretty, leafy ground cover.

Surprisingly, several of the more common ferns will put up with dry shade despite their lush-looking foliage, which suggests a preference for damp conditions. Look, in particular, for *Dryopteris filix-mas, Polystichum setiferum* and Polypodiums. For a contrast of foliage form, grow clumps of *Iris foetidissima*, which has arching sword-shaped evergreen leaves and, as a bonus, brilliant orange berries from late summer.

Water Gardens

*W*ater, more than any other garden feature, acts as an irresistible magnet for most people. Compare, for example, a rock garden with a water garden: there just isn't the same sort of fascination. You would hardly wander down the garden just to look at the rockery, but the sight and sound of water, the lushness of waterside foliage, and the to-ings and fro-ings of birds, dragonflies and other wildlife are all there begging to be admired.

From the practical point of view, a water theme is an especially good choice for the completely new garden. A pond can be a large feature and it is built instantly rather than having to wait for it to grow. Water plants, in any case, are notoriously fast-growing.

Try to keep at least half of the surface of your pond clear of plants and dark shadows. This will leave the rest clear to reflect the sky and the surrounding plants. Around the margins of your pool, choose subjects that will give a clear and definite reflection of both colour and form. Most bushy plants make poor reflections in water, whereas tall flowering spires and dramatic spiky-leaved plants work best.

Left: a formal pond set in a paved area at Tintinhull House in Somerset, is planted simply with Water Iris set in mesh containers resting on a ledge around the perimeter of the pond. And towards the centre, where the water is deeper, Water Lilies spread over the surface, though a large part of the pond is left clear so as to catch the reflections of the surroundings.

Right: *giant foliage plants, such as* Gunnera manicata *and* Lysichiton americanus, *can somehow give a sense of mystery to a water garden. Their huge size conjures up fantasy images of gnomes and pixies, or Alice in Wonderland perhaps.*

Below: *the stunning Arum lily,* Zantedeschia aethiopica *'Crowborough', makes a perfect waterside plant.*

Whether your water garden is to provide the main theme for your whole garden, or whether it is to be just an aspect of a main central theme, there are certain considerations special to water gardens and their plants.

The first is the character of the water itself, which is simultaneously about movement and stillness. The very flatness of the water's surface has a calming quality, and its reflections balance out the world, with its sky and plants, creating a sense of equilibrium. Yet a large part of the fascination of water is in watching it move. These twin characteristics of stillness and movement should be shown off to the full, whatever kind of water garden you're planning.

Ponds and water features can be either informal and naturalistic, or formal and self-evidently man-made. Whichever style you choose, if the pond is small you will probably need a pump to keep the water fresh and healthy. The best lining material for any type of pond is strong butyl rubber sheeting with a good thick layer of stone-free sand under it.

Opposite: *a small rivulet makes its way through rocky crevices edged by a cushion of purple Campanulas and a clump of moisture-loving Lady Fern (*Athyrium filix femina*). You don't need a natural stream to create this effect: all you need is a small pump to take the water back to the top of the watercourse.*

Natural-looking water features obviously need to be sited at the lowest point in your garden. Throw a long garden hose over the area where you want your pond – this should give you some natural curves to guide your excavations.

A natural-looking water's edge is the trickiest part to simulate. Hide the rubber lining with some carefully placed stones, some small spreading plants such as Creeping Jenny, and some larger shrubs and perennials like Willows and Dogwoods, bamboos, ferns, Hostas and Iris. All these plants will look very appropriate at the water's edge but they do not require the permanently boggy soil that would occur naturally in this situation.

A formal pond can be any regular shape – round, oval, rectangular, square or many-sided – and it

Above: *a natural-looking water feature is entirely in keeping with this country garden and provides a pleasant and peaceful spot in which to sit out.*

Opposite: *this circular pond has been allowed to become overgrown in order to make it appear less formal and more 'jungly', in keeping with the rest of the garden. One problem, however, is that the water will need dredging of duck weed soon if it is not to become unhealthy.*

may be level with the ground or raised, so that you can sit around its edge. A centrepiece like a fountain is an option in this style of pond, whereas it would look very inappropriate in a 'natural' setting.

Above: the low wall around this raised rectangular pond makes a nice cool spot for sitting on a hot day. Containerised plants will also welcome the moist atmosphere and break up the bare stonework. A small concealed pump circulates the water from the pond up to the bird bath.

Water plants grow very quickly, so a pond is a speedily established feature. Once a balance between its various inhabitants – both plant and animal – has been struck, it can easily be maintained, though it must be attended to regularly. To make the most of the water's movement, make sure that it is always kept clean. Then you will be able to see reflections glinting on the surface

A WATER GARDEN

The design of this formal water garden (below) *is based on the same principle as the one shown in the photograph, left. A low wall forms the edge of the pond and provides a useful place in which to put plants. Because the pond is raised and the lower end of the garden is also slightly elevated, the pond dominates the plot and* makes the whole garden seem rather grand. The paired urns, the central pathway neatly planted with Alchemilla, and the matching raised bed behind the pond all add to the formality and grandeur of the garden. The two grassed areas, with their mixed planting of shrubs, climbers and herbaceous plants, provide an attractive setting.

Wild Gardens

More and more is said and written about 'wild' gardens although, strictly speaking, this is a contradiction in terms. A garden is, by definition, the product of man's manipulation of nature.

What is usually meant by 'wild' is a style of garden which uses only native plants and a minimum of maintenance – perhaps no more than a twice-yearly mow. Unless you want to live in a wilderness, this theme is appropriate for only part of your garden – perhaps the very bottom area where it would feel like your own little piece of countryside. Make sure it is out of view from the house, since a 'wild' area can actually look awful outside the growing season.

Left: *this trampled rough grass path leads through an overgrown orchard, underplanted with naturalised spring bulbs.*

63

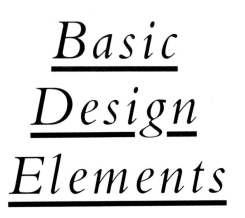

Basic Design Elements

Once you have subdivided your garden space and decided on a rough layout and a theme for each area, or for the whole garden, you can then consider the basic design in a little more detail. Should the sitting area be paved or gravel? Exactly how should the change in levels between two areas be achieved. What kind of path would be best? There is still no need to think about specific plants – unless, of course, you have some existing large plants that need to be 'built' into your plan.

A slightly raised sitting area gives a good view of the surrounding scenery. The old red brick wall supports climbers and wall shrubs but is still sufficiently visible to add its warm tones and set off the colour of the nearby foliage.

Paths and Paved Areas

Y our rough layout should have indicated the positioning of paths and paved areas and you should now consider their style and practicality in a little more detail. Paths to front doors need to be by the shortest route possible, since your visitors will soon create one there anyway. If possible, they should be well lit and not slippery when they're damp. There's nothing more unnerving and unwelcoming than a dark and dangerous front path. Within the garden itself, you can be a little less practical.

Left: *a lovely old cobbled path takes the visitor down to a hedged garden. The plants lining the pathway, such as pale pink, frothy London Pride (Saxifraga × urbium) and the large-leaved Bergenia, spill over and soften the path's straight edges.*

Opposite: *crushed bark makes a lovely informal pathway through a planted area.*

Above: *orange and bright green are complementary colours. Here Box hedging edges a red brick path to make a really clean, fresh line.*

Right: *grass would never grow very satisfactorily beneath these two old conifers and old flagstones glow beautifully in the dappled sunlight.*

The basic choice of material for hard surfaces is between brick, stone, gravel, concrete and wood. The easiest, and often the cheapest, to lay is gravel or stone chippings – though it can be a nuisance if it gets trampled into the house on people's shoes.

Concrete paving does not need to be as ghastly as it sounds but be sure to choose the type of paving slab that looks like concrete, not the terrible fake stone ones. Concrete paving looks most in keeping in a garden with a modern theme.

Brickwork comes in many styles and colours and is perhaps the most versatile hard surfacing, lending itself equally well to the herringboned brick path of a cottage garden and to the dark grey paving bricks of a sleek, ultra-modern garden.

Real stone paving always looks good, whether it is laid uniformly or randomly, as neat, regular-shaped slabs or irregular uneven pieces. It is, however, often the most expensive choice of material. Old stone paving is usually the best and, if you get the chance, try and buy it before it's been removed from its original site – then you can number the slabs and re-lay them in the same order so that it's wear looks natural.

The availability of different types of stone varies from one area to another, as do their colours – from quite pale whitish grey, through strong mustardy yellow, to handsome blue-black of slate.

Wood is another option worth considering, although it won't last for as long as stone or concrete. Stepping-stone sections of a tree

trunk can make a natural-looking path through a planted area, while horizontally laid sleepers can make a soft, dark 'paved' area. Slatted decking is another possibility but, although it's fine for verandahs, roof gardens and balconies, it somehow has a strangely temporary look.

Whatever material you choose, there are one or two important points to be observed when laying paths or paving. Firstly, allow a good depth for the foundations: at least 4in (10cm) of hardcore plus 4in (10cm) of sand on top to bed in the paving material. Secondly, make sure you don't pave above a building's damp course – if you have to, then line the wall with a waterproof material first. And finally, an expanse of paving should always be laid to a slight fall so that water can drain away,

Left: *concrete paving can look entirely appropriate in a modern setting, though it should not try to look like anything other than concrete.*

Below: *stone paving slabs softened by mossy tufts of* Sagina glabra *make an attractive stepping-stone path.*

Above: *irregularly shaped stone pieces laid roughly to a level and with no visible cement grouting are a far cry from awful suburban crazy-paving.*

Right: *the texture of pea-shingle is echoed in the choice of edging plants. On the left, Golden Marjoram shows its round, sulphurous young leaves; in the centre, the tight pebble-like buds of Santolina will fill out slightly as the summer progresses; and, on the right, the blue-grey, woolly foliage of Artemisia reiterates the grey softness of the stones.*

Above: *arching, strap-like leaves of Agapanthus are contrasted with delicate fern fronds, a tiny variegated Ivy and a bold clump of broad-leaved Bird's Nest Fern.*

Opposite: *this gravel path, provides a delightful walk through the Rose garden.*

Gravel is a splendid material to use among plants, particularly in a country-style garden. Apart from being relatively inexpensive and very easy to lay, it gives a much softer and more informal look than paving ever can. The natural shape and movement of a plant is not restricted or corseted by a gravel path in the same way that it is by paving – hence a freer, more fluid appearance that is much easier on the eye. This was recognised by the Japanese masters, who often used gravel to represent water and raked it into patterns to symbolise waves.

And, as gravel presents no limitation to the growth of plants below ground, it is perfectly possible to cover an entire planting area with a layer of gravel. This helps to keep down weeds as well as conserving soil moisture.

Changes In Level

O ne of the most effective ways
of adding interest to your garden
design is to incorporate a change
of level into the plan. Once you have decided
on the relative levels of the different areas of
your garden, then you have to consider how,
in practice, these changes should occur. The
design details will depend mainly on the
effect you're trying to create.

Right: *a pair of conifers stand guard on either side of
the entrance through to the rather grand raised terrace
– which is itself stepped, breaking up the large expanse
of lawn.*

Opposite: the curved steps in the background give the upper garden a really grand entrance, whereas the simple worn flagstones leading down through a narrow gap in the hedge suggest a secret garden in the foreground.

Above: a slight change in level gives this sitting area a good view of the garden. It is achieved by using timber sleepers to retain the planted area. Low-growing plants have been used so as to preserve the view.

Left: a mysterious cave-like feeling is created at the entrance to the upper garden by the use of rough-hewn rock steps leading into darkness. Alchemilla and ferns help to soften the stonework.

For a natural-looking area in a country garden, a simple grassy bank would be very appropriate. A path leading down to a dark and mysterious grotto garden might be of very narrow, steep steps, set into steep banks of large mossy rocks.

From a practical point of view, the raised bed is a useful device around which to plan a change in level. The simplest design is to keep the bed flush with the ground at the higher level, and to stop the soil from spilling out on to the lower level by a wall of some sort — creating a raised planting area. Steps cutting through from one area to another can be contained within the depth of the raised bed, or project into the lower garden.

Opposite: *the clean lines of the sunken garden give it a modern look. The rendered and painted walls reflect the light, set off the plants and add to the feeling of a room outside. In contrast, up the steps is the busy clutter of a Victorian-style town garden.*

Above: *a change in levels can be an opportunity to change mood and style. From this light and airy informal garden, step down to this severe monastic cloister where Ivies, ferns and Hostas enjoy the moist shaded conditions.*

For a grander scheme you could have a stepped bed, with one or more terraces between the higher and lower gardens. To make an area seem both private from the inside and a little intriguing from the outside, you can use a garden divider such as a trellis, wall or hedge.

A change in level or indeed any kind of earth-moving usually requires a considerable amount of effort and can cause absolute chaos while the operation is in progress. Don't be put off, though, since once the job is done you will never need to do it again – your garden will soon settle down and, if it has been well thought out, will have a very firm basic structure. Do plan ahead, though, and know exactly what levels you want where. Remove the top soil, putting it carefully aside. Move the subsoil to achieve the levels you want, then spread the top soil over it.

Above: a leafy garden, predominantly green and yellow, has been created here using masses of Hostas, frothy Alchemilla mollis *in the foreground, and elegant yellow Day-lilies, with arching strap-shaped foliage. The ground between the plants is paved with gravel and old York stone, the latter tinged green with a layer of algae which, although it may be visually in keeping, unfortunately makes a lethal slippery surface in wet weather.*

The design of the garden should always bear some relation to that of the house. A visual link, such as the positioning of a garden archway directly in line with an internal arch, will make the garden truly belong to the house – an association that will help to create an atmosphere of ease and relaxation in both house and garden. Always try and incorporate some design detail of the house into the garden hardware, even if it is only to use the same type of brick. A lot of older houses have little decorative bits of stonework – like scrolls or festoons. Try and use similar decorations on garden pillars, walls or archways.

A TWO-LEVEL GARDEN

This split-level garden reflects the foliage theme illustrated in the photograph, left, and supplements it with a small herb garden set in gravel. Leaf forms vary from large, dramatic ones, like the Fatsia japonica *in the pot by the right-hand bench, Hostas beneath the trees, and the trees themselves – the Indian Bean Tree (Catalpa bignonioides) at the bottom of the garden, and the Fig tree halfway down – to the feathery foliage like yellow-flowered* Santolina incana *(in the pot beside the Fatsia) and several different ferns.*

In this garden plan (below), a basement room has necessitated the change in level in the garden design, which mirrors the width of the room inside. This layout not only ties the house to the garden but also provides a very private outdoor eating area close to the house.

Garden Seating

A garden seat is more than just somewhere to relax and admire the view. It is actually part of the scene itself, so as much care should be taken in its choice and positioning as with any other garden feature.

Styles and materials are virtually limitless – from the good old-fashioned wood and canvas deckchair to the rare antique stone seats sometimes obtainable from architectural salvage companies or auction rooms. Choose a material that can happily stay out in all weathers, or that even improves with the green tinge of moss or algae.

Above: *a garden bench becomes an arbour beneath the cascade of a large-flowered hybrid Clematis.*

Far left: *the textural quality of the orange-tinted foliage of this* Acer palmatum *'Dissectum' cultivar is matched by the ridged texture of the blue bench.*

Above left: *imagine this pergola without the chair beneath it – it gives meaning to the whole scene.*

Left: *stone and concrete mellow with age as they acquire a population of mosses and algae. A garden bench like this one is often regarded as purely ornamental, but a plentiful supply of canvas cushions will encourage sitters.*

Above right: *concrete makes a good substitute for stone and, as it ages, it becomes harder to distinguish between the two. These concrete pots filled with colourful cottage-garden flowers are set off in the background by a gorgeous purple-leaved Grape Vine.*

Above: *a lovely pedestal container brings some height to this pink and grey scheme. Ivy-leaved Geraniums are very useful for tumbling out of tall containers.*

Far right: *traditional terracotta pots of Geraniums queue up on either side of these steps.*

Right: *Sissinghurst's Chamomile seat proves that you can make a plant container out of anything.*

Plants In Containers

P lants in pots and containers of every kind can furnish a paved or gravel garden which would otherwise look barren and lifeless. Apart from the obvious advantages of being moveable if you change houses, a container garden has a number of advantages over a conventional one.

Most significantly, you, the gardener, are in total control of your contained plants. You choose their soil which, after all, does bear their nutrient and water supply. You choose, and can alter, their position – and thus their shelter and light conditions.

The size of container – its depth and the amount of soil it contains will also affect the ultimate size of your plants. So are you up to the job? A terrace packed with marvellous and healthy-looking plants, spilling over the tops of their pots, looks great but to achieve this you must attend to them regularly.

Most plants are happy growing in containers – bulbs, herbaceous perennials, shrubs, climbers, even trees – as long as they are supplied with the right amount of water and nutrients. The most easily grown container plants, however, are those that will tolerate a wide range of soil moisture conditions – from very dry to waterlogged – since these extremes are commonly found at one time or another in all contained soil.

Above: *a dense curtain of climbers and shrubs gives this garden privacy but also casts shade. Containerised plants are relatively movable, so you can shuffle your pots around to give them all a turn in the light. The relaxed yet sophisticated atmosphere is created here with a lovely collection of old and new containers. Among the plants is a handsome, large-leaved Hosta, a magnificent cut-leaved Maple, and a pot of Lilies that, although past their best and a little messy, are still wonderfully elegant.*

Large expanses of paving can look extremely bleak without a few groups of pots and urns to break up the stark lines. The choice of containers and the plants that go in them are obviously determined by your design theme, but there are a few points to remember with any potted outdoor plants.

Tall thin containers, like chimney pots or pedestal urns, for example, always need a cascading plant to link the plant visually with its pot. Do not be tempted, with very large, wide-necked containers, to crowd in too many different plants, as this always looks a mess. It's rarely advisable to use more than three different plants in the same pot.

You can move containers about at will. In fact, one way of decorating a very dark area is to rotate your pots, so that they all do a short stretch in the dark. And lastly, remember that potted plants are not the same as those growing in the garden. You have to play substitute for a free root run to supply them with sufficient air, water and nourishment. Good drainage, regular watering and feeding are all vitally important to healthy and attractive pot plants.

A CONTAINER GARDEN

In this container garden (below), gravel covers the ground, giving a soft old-fashioned look Almost everything is 'contained' in some way: raised beds contain climbers that clothe the backdrop of walls and fences; there is a miniature pond contained in an old ceramic sink; and a secret garden, based on the one in the photograph, left, encloses a corner of the garden, providing a private, shaded haven during hot weather.

Scarlet, crimson and salmon-pink climbing Roses grow in containers and clamber together over walls and trelliswork. In the top left-hand corner, a large-leaved tree, Catalpa bignonioides, helps create some privacy and is one of the few plants here growing out of the ground. And Irish Ivy, Hedera helix 'Hibernica', creeps over the gravel. Ox-eye Chamomile, Anthemis tinctoria, spills out of the stone pot beside the bench. The bottom right-hand corner garden is the focal point of the garden from the sitting room windows: a Snake Bark Maple, Acer capillipes, has been chosen for this spot, since its attractive bark and well-defined rounded shape make it of all-year-round interest. Pebbles mulch the soil in the tree's raised bed and more Irish Ivy creeps over the ground.

Above right: *this unlikely chap gives some point to a shady corner of ferns and climbing Hydrangea.*

Above: *a beautiful old stone ornament brings a little classical grandeur to the top of a wall.*

Far right: *the somewhat skeletal structure of this modern sculpture is reflected in the open branching of the white-flowered* Crambe cordifolia.

Right: *a head half-glimpsed round a hedge makes an intriguing view, inviting onlookers to explore the garden further.*

Garden Ornaments

*P*eople often shy away from using ornaments in the garden. They are such an obvious statement of personal taste, whereas plants are to some extent responsible for their own existence and may somehow seem to have visited themselves upon you. Sculptures and other objects are, however, invaluable in garden design since, in contrast to all around them, they remain unchanged through the seasons and (apart from a little weathering) the years. Thus they provide stability and continuity among an ever-changing and growing collection of plants.

Colour
Planning

Colour is the most important factor to contribute to the overall effect of a planting plan. There are many complicated theories and confusing terms applied to colour and how it works – most of them not very helpful since they don't take into account texture or translucency.

There are, however, one or two useful guidelines to bear in mind when choosing a colour scheme for a garden. The best solution for a small space is usually one basic colour plus a few related shades and tones of it. Where a group of very similar colours have been used, small patches or spots of other, strongly contrasting, deeper-toned colour may work well as an accent.

For a long flower border, it is useful to remember that white, yellows, oranges and reds all tend to 'jump out' at you, whereas purples, blues and greens tend to recede. Thus it is best to emphasise depth by using the retreating colours in the background, and the advancing ones in the foreground.

White Flowers and Gardens

*W*hite gardens are by far the most popular of the colour-theme gardens – inspired perhaps by Vita Sackville-West's interpretation at Sissinghurst (see page 36). The reason that white works so well is perhaps because it has an extremely dramatic effect: at the same time as being soft and soothing, many white flowers massed together have a sort of magical, fairyland quality. None of this, of course, would be possible without the fact that an enormous range of plants have white flowers – from the most delicate papery Sweet Peas to the richest velvety Arum Lilies – so there are always plenty of species to choose from.

Leaf colours and textures are especially well set off by white flowers, so a white garden with a 'sub-theme' of contrasting foliage would work extremely well. Try lime-green ferns with silvery Lavender or Santolina and plum-coloured Cotinus 'Royal purple', dotted with white Lilies all set among clouds of starry white Gypsophila. Don't worry about the odd spots of colour given by the flowers of 'foliage' plants – these often add to, rather than detract from, the effect. Alternatively, if you're feeling really pedantic, or simply dislike the effect, you can always pick any non-white flowers for the house before they open fully.

Left: *white-tinged-with-green Agapanthus flowers are carried high above their clumps of strap-shaped mid-green .*

93

Right: *in this 'wild' hedge bottom, intriguing flashes of yellow, blue, mauve and pink flowers among the grasses are crowned by a delicate white froth of Cow Parsley.*

Right: *once you've drunk in the wonderful scent of summer-flowering Jasmine, even a photograph is mouth-watering.*

Left: *Trilliums make delightful ground-cover plants for moist, rich soil in dappled woodland shade. Their simple but beautiful white flowers appear in late spring or early summer.*

Above: *when is white not really white? The marvellous thing about white as a colour theme is that you can veer between many different 'whites' – flowers may be distinctly tinged with yellow, green, blue or pink, or they may just reflect that colour very subtly in the folds and shadows of their petals. Creamy white Rosa 'Nevada' looks increasingly yellow towards the centre, as its petals pick up the reflection of the golden stamens.*

Right: Viburnum plicatum *is a fabulous shrub with a spectacular tiered arrangement of branches and many clusters of pure white late spring flowers.*

Above: *stunning pure white Azaleas can give a really snowy effect in the spring when their branches are laden with blossoms.*

Left: *the arrangement of leaves and bracts of the woolly white Stachys echoes the colour and triangular shapes of the beautiful Iris behind.*

Yellow Flowers and Gardens

Yellow means sunshine: it is a warm, cheerful, often not very subtle colour that can make you feel like smiling. Mixed with cream and white, yellow becomes much softer and more sophisticated and creates an altogether more relaxing picture.

To many people, yellow epitomises spring but, used alone, it can so easily become too hot a colour. Mix it with white to keep the picture cool, fresh and optimistic, like glorious springtime weather.

Yellow flowers are some of the most popular and best known. Start the year in deepest winter with winter Jasmine, Witch Hazel and Winter Sweet: all have their bare branches spangled with small, cheerful yellow blossoms. As spring progresses, the bulbs come into their own, from delicate miniature species of Daffodils to large, brassy Crown Imperials. Late spring and early summer bring Laburnum and, of course, plenty of young yellow-green foliage, like the golden-leaved False Acacia, which glows like a beacon in the sunshine.

Among the summer yellows are innumerable Lilies, Daisies and many yellow-flowered shrubs, like Santolina, Senecio and Potentillas. Autumn often sees Witch Hazel foliage turning to a rich yellow, giving this plant a double role for the yellow garden.

Left: a colourful ribbon of bright yellow Welsh poppies dances gaily among ground-covering foliage. Allow them to self-seed every year then they'll eventually pop up throughout your beds and borders.

Right: *the spidery summer daisy flowers of Inula enjoy a sunny position in any reasonable garden soil.*

Below: *a tough, summer-flowering perennial that grows like a weed and needs no attention, Loosestrife (Lysimachia punctata) is ideal for naturalising in wild areas. Don't use it in an ordinary border though, or it may take over.*

Right: *although they make the perfect spring bulb for an exotic 'jungle' theme, these dramatic Crown Imperials can look out of place in some settings.*

Opposite: *classic daisy flowers, like this bushy low-growing Feverfew, are very useful in predominantly yellow colour schemes. Thus the splashes of white effectively lift and lighten the rich buttery flowers of these Potentillas.*

Above: *the beautiful, velvety, sun-loving daisy flowers of Dimorphotheca also come in many other colours. They'll make a spreading mound of daisies from early summer until the first frosts.*

Left: *Alchemilla mollis is one of the most useful and attractive garden plants. A shade-tolerant gap filler without being invasive, it has delightful long-lived yellow flowers, seen here echoing the dense yellow clusters of Achillea.*

Opposite: *cream variegated plants, like this potted Acer negundo, are very valuable for providing a visual link between yellow flowers and green foliage.*

103

Orange Flowers and Gardens

O range is the hottest colour of all. With no trace of coolness in its make-up, orange has blue as its opposite. They are both intense hues, yet blue is a strongly receding colour and orange an advancing one, so it is a good idea to exaggerate the perspective by combining the two. In spring, orange can look brassy and out of place. Summer and autumn are the best seasons for orange, when you can create a new effect each year with temporary bedding plants, such as Snap Dragons, Gazanias, even Nasturtiums.

Marigolds last the entire summer, thrive on the poorest soil and will keep the greenfly away, so before you turn your nose up at this much-maligned plant look through the seed catalogues. The small-flowered French Marigolds can look particularly effective among rich, dark green or sharp lime-green foliage. Pot Marigolds (Calendula officinalis) are very pretty for a cottage-garden look and can be picked for summer salads. Lilies are perhaps the most beautiful of the orange perennials. They lend an exotic emphasis to an orange colour scheme. There are many different Lilies available – from the bright, cheerful 'Enchantment' Lilies to the more delicate 'Turk's Cap' types.

Left: for a softer and more gentle contrast, use orange with a slightly purple blue – in other words a blue with a little warmth in it – which is a colour combination found in a single Iris flower.

Above: *the clear, warm tangerine-orange of Pot Marigolds, a traditional cottage-garden flower used in cooking and as a medicinal herb.*

Right: *sprays of flame-coloured, beautiful Turk's Cap Lilies hang their heads towards the sun.*

Above: *among the relatively few orange-flowered shrubs are some fabulous Rhododendrons – here adding a touch of the exotic to a dense wall of mature greenery.*

Left: *don't despise Pansies just because park keepers are so fond of them. This burnished copper-coloured variety makes an excellent combination with silver-leaved Cineraria.*

Above: *for a softer effect, tone down orange by mixing it with yellow and cream. Pale coppery orange Alstroemeria merge with yellow Pansies, while a few bright purple ones add a little accidental but effective contrast.*

Right: *bold, cup-shaped orange Poppy flowers give the impression of floating in mid-air, as their thin, wiry stems seem to bear no relation to them.*

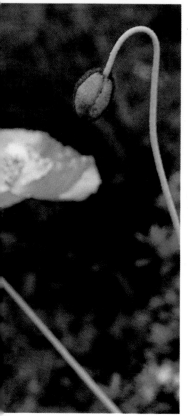

Above: *these Chinese Lanterns will develop and continue their orange glow from late summer until well into the autumn.*

Red Flowers and Gardens

*P*assionate and fiery or regal and dignified, red could be said to be the turning point between hot and cool colours: scarlet is still burning hot whereas maroon is distinctly cool.

Given that mid-green–the colour of most foliage – is its complementary colour, red can make a very dramatic and effective single-colour theme for a garden.

The best range of red flowers appears in the summer, although it is possible to have red flowers throughout the year. In winter and early spring, the gorgeous Camellia japonica 'Adolphe Audusson' is one of several red Camellia varieties.

Later on in the spring, a Japanese Quince like Chaenomeles speciosa 'Kermesina Plena' makes a glorious wall shrub with glowing scarlet flowers. Blood-red Wallflowers and crimson Tulips bridge the period between spring and early summer when maroon Peonies and a wide range of beautifully coloured Poppies start to appear.

The autumn brings rich red tints to many plants. Virginia Creeper and Boston Ivy both make great backdrops for a red border, as both are a beautiful rich green in summer and complement the red summer flowers, then reliably turn any shade of red from scarlet to mahogany in autumn.

Left: *Geraniums (or, more properly, Pelargoniums) are the classic red flowers of summer. Shown here is a rich and exotic collection of scarlet, salmon and pink varieties, all wonderfully set off by glossy, green Ivy foliage.*

Above: *Azaleas come in many colours, including this intense bluish red. The surrounding dark, lime-green foliage is close to its complementary colour and so makes a clean and stylish contrast.*

Right: *a rich crimson Clematis cascading down a wall makes a lovely backdrop for a red border.*

Above: *dark red makes a good solid background to a mainly yellow scheme, as yellow 'advances' the red. Touches of orange here would ease and soften the contrast.*

Left: *red fruits can extend the colour season right through the winter – though some, like these shining scarlet Rose Hips, will stay for only a few weeks.*

Above: *bright red Poppies stand to attention among tall, pinkish red Ornamental Rhubarb flowers.*

Right: *royal blue railings bring out the blue in these maroon Tobacco plants, making a surprising and pleasing colour mix.*

Opposite: *this scorching hot scarlet creeper, Tropaeolum speciosum, adds to the exotic, jungly effect by clambering up through large, leafy shrubs.*

Pink Flowers and Gardens

The colour pink is soft and warm. It ranges from mauve in one direction to orange in the other – a good point to remember when it comes to choosing 'accent' plants. Pink itself is useful in that it provides gentle, muted background colour, which is well set off by most foliage colours – dark green, lime-green or even maroon – but beware the combination of gold leaves and pink flowers.

The range is enormous and the choice is especially good among old-fashioned cottage-garden flowers: from the palest winter-flowering Cherries and Camellias, through a summer of creamy pink Peonies, sweet-smelling Stocks and a host of marvellous Roses, right up until the autumn when elegant Nerines, icy pink autumn Crocus and tiny woodland Cyclamen appear.

Right: *Felicia is a lovely old shrub Rose that can either be trained against a trellis or left free standing as an arching bush; masses of these exquisitely scented flowers appear during early and mid-summer; the delicate pink slowly turns to ivory as the flowers fade.*

Right: *an easy-going, shade-tolerant evergreen ground covering plant,* Polygonum bistorta *makes a continuous mat of foliage with long-lived flowers in pale or dark pink from summer until autumn.*

Left: *there are few more heart-warming sights than that of clear spring sunshine sparkling through the palest pink Cherry blossom.*

Left: *'Lacecap' Hydrangeas are often far prettier than their 'Mophead' sisters. Remember, when choosing your varieties, that the colour of Hydrangea flowers depends partly on your soil and you can, to some extent, adjust this: if your pink varieties have turned purple, add some ground limestone to the soil.*

Above: *pink is not always a warm colour; these Autumn Crocus, for example, have a decidedly icy feel.*

Right: *a riot of pinks ranges from nearly red, through orange and mauve, to not quite white. Rhododendron varieties come in all shades and make a fabulous display in late spring.*

Above: *sugary pink Roses are set off by the lime-green umbels of Angelica.*

Left: *a softer contrast can be achieved using colours that are not exact complementaries. Here, the two greens lie on either side of khaki, which is the true complementary colour to pink.*

Purple Flowers and Gardens

*P*urple is one of the best colours around which to plan a garden colour scheme; firstly because there are so many plants with purple flowers, and secondly because the colour covers such a wide range of tones and tints — mauve, lilac, lavender, violet and so on. Its opposite colours are, of course, equally wide-ranging: acid greens, creams and yellows. Purple also has a receding nature, making it a very useful background colour and giving it a quiet, restful and dignified mood when used alone.

Winter and spring see carpets of tiny pale purple woodland Cyclamen, followed by the showier deep mauve dwarf bulbous Iris and Crocus and the dark pinkish purple Hellebores. Later on in the year, in high summer, purple-flowered shrubs include the magical butterfly bush, Buddleia, and the Hebes — a useful group of attractive, neatly cushion-shaped evergreen shrubs. Lavender, Catmint and Heathers are all good smaller summer shrubs. Purple-flowered herbaceous plants are very common: Foxgloves, Lupins, the tall, handsome Acanthus, fluffy Liatris stems, and the very reliable and easy-going, mop-headed garden Phlox, to name just a few. And, of course, you can round off the year in autumn with large clumps of Michaelmas Daisies in every shade of purple, from mauve-pink to violet-blue.

Left: *late spring and early summer bring a fabulous range of bearded Iris — useful not only for their flowers but also for their dramatic sword-shaped leaves, shown here with purple Ornamental Onion flowers.*

Above: *purple Catmint (Nepeta) fills out the front of a bed of tall lime-green Angelica.*

Right: *the unlikely association of a mauve Clematis with scarlet Tropaeolum speciosum against clear white paintwork makes an eye-catching combination.*

Opposite: *magenta Lupins make a smart, stylish show against their crisp green foliage.*

Above: *lilac Aquilegias make an easy-going if somewhat untidy cottage-garden plant. Both single- and bi-coloured varieties are available.*

Top: *a cloud of palest purple* Calamentha nepatioides *spills over and softens the lines of this garden path.*

Left: *a luminous, lime-green fern sets off its pink and pale purple partners,* Hesperis matronalis, *which has a beautiful scent in the evenings.*

Opposite: *a dark conifer background is cheered by a dense foam of pinky mauve Phlox, grouped behind paler pinks and greys.*

Blue Flowers and Gardens

*B*lue can bring a cool and misty atmosphere to a garden – especially when used alone or combined with purple, pink or white. Soft, romantic and beautiful as it is, true blue is in fact very rare as a flower colour.

For blue flowers from spring until the autumn, you can start the season with intense, deep blue spring-flowering Gentians (like Gentiana acaulis) or purple-blue Anemone blanda. *In later spring, both Forget-me-nots and Bluebells will smother the ground with a heart-stopping mist of blue, just as that magnificent blue wall shrub,* Ceanothus impressus, *covers walls and fences with its delicate powder-blue blossom. Elegant spires of Veronica flowers come in several true-blue shades – from pale sky to deep ultramarine – and will flower some time between spring and mid-summer. Then in early to mid-summer, blue spires such as Delphiniums, Campanula, Monkshood and Salvia, take the stage.*

Annuals, such as Flax, Cornflowers, Love-in-a-mist and Lobelia, are useful blue-flowered gap-fillers. In the autumn, vivid blue Gentiana × macaulayi, stylish Agapanthus and a later-flowering Ceanothus such as 'Gloire de Versailles' draw the final curtain over the blue garden.

Right: *no blue summer garden would be complete without its stand of fabulous huge Himalayan blue poppies. None of the blue Meconopsis is an easy plant to grow, but they are nevertheless well worth trying.*

Right: *if you're lucky enough to live in a frost-free area, or you have some space in your greenhouse or conservatory, try growing the palest sky-blue Plumbago, a stunning summer-flowering climber.*

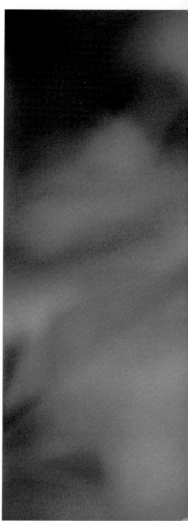

Above: *the regal, majestic Delphinium, king of the summer perennials, comes in several rich, glowing shades of blue and purple.*

Right: *choose the Periwinkle for fast-growing, evergreen ground cover, with inky blue flowers in summer.*

Far right: *plant some clumps of Monkshood (Aconitum) among your Delphiniums to extend the season of blue flowering spires.*

130

Right: *soft, faded, purple-blue 'Mophead' Hydrangeas billowing frothily behind a clump of bright pink Astilbes.*

Left: *a heavenly haze of Forget-me-nots provides a startling ground cover around these clipped Yew tree benches.*

Left: *white and green variegated Dogwood and dusty grey-leaved Sage bring out the lilac in this powder-blue Ceanothus.*

Green Plants and Gardens

Green obviously provides the background colour for almost all planting schemes. The colour green varies enormously, though: from the creamy, golden, and lime-greens of plants like Alchemilla mollis *and the variegated* Tolmiea; *through the blue and greyish greens of Rue and Artemis, the bronze greens of Mahonia in autumn and the dusty pinkish greens of some variegated Sages and Fuchsias; to the dark almost black greens of many Yews and Hollies, not to mention the numerous shades of honest-to-goodness light, mid and dark greens of the great majority of garden plants.*

Green offers great scope as a single-colour garden design theme. Foliage-only gardens also offer interesting design possibilities; these could include the yellow, red, maroon and purple leaf colours as well as the contrasting textures of non-flowering plants such as mosses, ferns, grasses, bamboos and conifers.

Left: *green is not restricted to foliage colours. There are also several green or green-tinged blossoms, such as Angelica (shown here), Moluccella, Nicotiana and some of the Hellebores.*

Above: *the round, umbrella-like leaves of Gunnera and the elongated ones of Lysichiton grow up through the leafy undergrowth.*

Left: *a rich pattern of contrasting leaf colours, shapes and textures is created in this foliage association.*

Top left: *the rounded young leaves of Golden Marjoram contrast with the fine foliage and tiny yellow flower buds of Santolina virens.*

Far left: *the shape of the small, glossy, leaves of Abelia is echoed in the large, felty, leaves of Pulmonaria.*

137

The Plant Catalogue

Once you've decided on the theme and layout for your garden, you will then need to choose the plants that you want to fill the beds and borders. To simplify this problem, some of the best plants have been categorised in the following pages into a few basic shapes. Build up repeating patterns with these shapes to create an interesting picture, then choose which plants you want for each shape. Your repeating-shape patterns need not always be represented by the same plants – you can vary your choice if you want to create a less formal and more complex planting scheme.

Lupinus Polyphyllus

Lysimachia Nummularic

Lilium Tigrinum

Tropaeloum

Hedera Helix 'Goldheart'

Large Trees

No garden should be without at least one large tree. Apart from providing a magnificent focus of attention, a large tree can be useful in screening an ugly view – or indeed obscuring your neighbours' view of you. The trees listed will generally grow taller than 20ft (6m), though they are not necessarily enormous. They will, however, become a major feature in any garden.

BETULA PENDULA Silver Birch
Green foliage in summer

A lovely tree with spreading then arching branches and a filigree of small olive-green leaves (30 × 15ft.9m × 4.5m). The stark white bark and the wonderful tree shape mean that it's pretty all year round. *B.p. 'Youngii',* Young's Weeping Birch, is usually a little smaller and more weeping.
□ Ordinary garden soil in sun or shade. Don't plant close to buildings or regularly dug flower beds, as it has wide spreading surface roots.
□ Looks lovely in a lawn, underplanted with white spring bulbs.

CORNUS NUTTALLII Dogwood
White flowers in late spring; yellow or red foliage in autumn

A beautiful flowering tree. Upright with arching branches that turn up at the tips (25 × 15ft / 7.5 × 4.5m). Lovely creamy white flowers cover the leafless branches in late spring. Foliage turns yellow or red in autumn before falling.
□ Rich, moist but well-drained soil in sun or partial shade.
□ Allow plenty of space in which to show off in spring. Underplant with *Cornus canadensis* or *Trilliums* as ground cover, both of which have similar creamy white flowers.

EUCALYPTUS Gum Tree
Grey-blue foliage all year

This elegant fast-growing tree is tall and sinuous, and often a bit lop-sided. It has attractive dappled grey bark and is evergreen with two distinct foliage forms on the same tree – 'juvenile' and 'adult'. *Eucalyptus gunnii* (60 × 20ft / 18 × 6m) has silvery blue, round juvenile foliage which gives way on older wood to blue-green, sickle-shaped adult leaves. Can also be grown as a lovely grey-leaved shrub (6 × 4ft / 1.8 × 1.2m) if cut back to near ground level every year in late spring, in which case it will produce only juvenile foliage. *Eucalyptus niphophila*, the Snow Gum (30 × 15ft / 9 × 4.5m), is a tall, shapely, spreading tree. It produces blue-grey, lance-shaped, adult leaves which flutter prettily in the wind. Its lovely blotchy bark looks almost as if someone had splashed the trunk with white, grey and pale cream paint. Eucalyptus doesn't like to be moved, so always buy a container-grown tree. A small 12in (30cm) sapling can reach 15ft (4.5m) in three years, so it won't be small for long.
□ Moist but well-drained soil in full sun and sheltered from strong winds.
□ One of the best grey foliage plants, it looks lovely with rusty orange, yellow, pink, mauve or white. Excellent for screening your garden.

FICUS CARICA
Fig
Green leaves in summer

A handsome, large-leaved, spreading tree (30 × 25ft / 9 × 7.5m) with arching branches that turn up at the tip. The Fig's shape and its lovely grey wrinkled trunk – rather like an elephant's leg – make it just as attractive in winter as in summer.
□ Ordinary well-drained garden soil in full sun or partial shade.
□ Make a feature of a free-standing tree or train it flat against a sunny wall for a lovely fruiting wall shrub, though the fruit may not ripen. Also suitable for growing in a large container or raised bed.

LIQUIDAMBAR STYRACIFLUA
Sweet Gum
Orange and scarlet leaves in autumn

A splendid spreading conical tree (25 × 15ft / 7.5 × 4.5m) that turns from mid-green to brilliant orange and red in autumn.
□ Well-drained but moist soil in full sun or partial shade, sheltered from cold winds.
□ Makes a fabulous focal point in a large lawn.

PRUNUS
Pink or white flowers in spring; orange and red leaves in autumn

Some of the large Prunus species are very beautiful in spring and autumn and quite fast-growing. *Prunus dulcis*, the Ornamental Almond, (20 × 20ft / 6 × 6m) makes a lovely spreading tree with pale pink blossom in mid-spring. *Prunus 'Tai Haku'*, the Great White Cherry, (30 × 25ft / 9 × 7.5m) is a magnificent sight in mid-spring, when its clusters of large single white flowers appear with young copper-tinged leaves. *Prunus sargentii* (30 × 25ft / 9 × 7.5m) is an excellent choice if you want a major

Large Trees

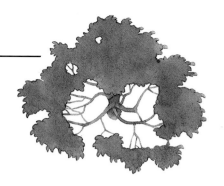

feature in a smallish garden. It makes a rounded, spreading canopy of branches which are covered with pale pink single flowers in mid-spring. In early autumn, the mid-green foliage reliably turns every shade of orange and red before falling. *Prunus serrula* (30 × 10ft / 9 × 3m) has branches that point upwards. Its main beauty lies in its gleaming mahogany-coloured polished bark.

☐ Ordinary garden soil in sun or partial shade.
☐ Makes a lovely feature in a lawn or set into paving.

ROBINIA PSEUDOACACIA 'FRISIA' False Acacia
Lime-green leaves in summer

One of the best trees for a gloomy town garden, as its leaves throw a brilliant golden green light when the sun shines through them. It has a lovely upright spreading shape (30 × 15ft / 9 × 4.5m) and creamy white flowers in summer.

☐ Ordinary garden soil in sun or partial shade.
☐ An excellent tree for planting in a paved area.

Small Trees

*To give an arrangement of plants a focal point or some instant height,
a tree that will reach no more than about 20ft (6m) is often the right choice.
Here are a few good small trees which are excellent for different purposes: their
autumn colour, their spring blossom, or perhaps their characteristic shape.
Any of these elements may give them a valuable role in your planting scheme.*

ACER Maple
Green, yellow, purple, red or variegated leaves in summer; orange, red or yellow leaves in autumn

This is a wonderful group of trees – among the loveliest in shape and leaf colour. *Acer davidii* (15 × 10ft / 4.5 × 3m) is a very attractive spreading tree with bright green, red-stalked leaves that turn yellow in autumn and beautiful green-grey and white striped bark. *A. griseum*, the Paper Bark Maple (15 × 10ft / 4.5 × 3m), has rusty, cinnamon-coloured peeling bark and widely spreading branches with mid-green leaves that turn vivid scarlet in autumn. The slow-growing *A. japonicum* includes several varieties, differing mainly in leaf shape and colour. Most will grow as a multi-stemmed bush or, if pruned, into a single-stemmed tree. *A. japonicum 'Aureum'* (20 × 15ft / 6 × 4.5m) makes an elegant spreading tree, with glowing, almost sulphurous yellow foliage which, like all *Acer japonicum* varieties, turns rich red in autumn before falling. *A. negundo*, the Box Elder (25 × 20ft / 7.5 x 6m), grows much faster than other small maples. It makes a spreading, bushy, round-headed tree with bright green leaves. There are several different varieties, of which *A.n. 'Variegatum'* has light green leaves with white margins and is ideal for brightening up a gloomy corner. *A. palmatum* (20 × 15ft / 6 × 4.5m) has many lovely slow-growing varieties – the *A.p. 'Dissectum'* group are particularly good-looking.

☐ Although they will tolerate some alkalinity, most Acers prefer a moist acid soil (without lime or chalk). Choose a sheltered site, away from cold winds and late spring frosts.
☐ These elegant trees are very beautiful, even without their leaves; draw attention to this in winter and early spring by underplanting with small low-growing bulbs like Scillas or Snowdrops.

BUDDLEIA ALTERNIFOLIA
Lavender-blue flowers in June

Not to be confused with the ordinary Buddleia, this makes a beautiful weeping tree (15 × 15ft / 4.5 × 4.5m) with elegant sinuous branches covered in mid-summer with round clusters of small lavender-blue flowers.

☐ Ordinary garden soil and full sun. To maintain a single stem, remove any side shoots as they appear.
☐ Makes a stunning focal point. Plant only low ground cover around the base so that the shape of the plant can be seen to good effect.

CATALPA BIGNONIOIDES
Indian Bean Tree
White flowers in summer

A round-headed tree (20 × 15ft / 6 × 4.5m) with large, handsome, light green leaves and clusters of

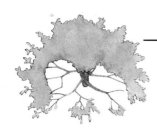

Small Trees

white orchid-like flowers in summer followed by long bean pods.
☐ Ordinary garden soil in sunny sheltered position.
☐ Gives height and shade to a flower border, but also makes a good enough shape to stand alone as a focal point.

FAGUS SYLVATICA 'PURPUREA PENDULA'
Weeping Purple Beech
Maroon-black leaves in summer

A small, mushroom-shaped, weeping tree (10 × 6ft /3 × 1.8m) with very dark maroon leaves.
☐ Ordinary well-drained garden soil, ideally sheltered from strong winds.
☐ Looks great with scarlet, mauve or yellow flowers and among lime-green or grey foliage.
☐ See also *Fatsia japonica*, Tiered Shrubs, page 149.

LABURNUM X WATERERI 'VOSSII'
Yellow flowers in late spring

An upright spreading tree (15 × 10ft/4.5 × 3m) with bright yellow spring flowers and light green leaves.
☐ Ordinary garden soil in sun or partial shade.
☐ There are three stunning ways of growing this tree: train it over an archway so that you walk under a canopy of gold and lime green; train a white Wisteria up the tree's stem to give fantastic cascades of gold and white blossom; use it to give height to a bright yellow and gold late spring border.
Poisonous, so keep away from children.

MAGNOLIA
White or purple-pink and white flowers in spring and summer

A magnificent tree with beautiful big velvety flowers. Buy the largest specimen you can afford as they are mostly slow-growing and tend not to flower when young. *Magnolia grandiflora* (15 × 10ft/ 4.5 × 3m) is a spreading evergreen with bright green leathery leaves, rusty underneath. Large creamy white flowers are produced intermittently throughout the summer and early autumn.
Magnolia soulangiana is a wide-spreading, deciduous

tree (15 × 15ft/4.5 × 4.5m), sometimes multi-stemmed like a giant shrub. Before the leaves appear in spring it is covered in huge white flowers; varieties with purple-flushed flowers are also available.
☐ Prefers a lime-free soil but will tolerate lime if the soil is rich, moist and well drained. Shelter from cold winds and frosts, ideally in a sunny position.
☐ Can be grown either free-standing or as a large wall shrub. Grow alone or with low ground-covering plants like Bergenia. Can also be grown in a container.

MALUS SYLVESTRIS
Apple
White blossom in spring

Many species of Malus are available but the most beautiful is undoubtedly the ordinary edible Apple This comes in several varieties, any of which will make a lovely small tree. Choose 'Standard' (15 × 15ft/4.5 × 4.5m) or 'Half-standard' (12 × 12 ft/3.6 × 3.6m) sizes (rather than 'Dwarf' or 'Bush') for a decent-sized tree with masses of late spring white blossom and, of course, plenty of apples in autumn.
☐ Ordinary garden soil in sunny position, sheltered from cold winds and late spring frosts.
☐ The loveliest way to grow apples is in an 'orchard' – a minimum of three trees, underplanted with grass dotted with meadow flowers.

PRUNUS
Ornamental Almond, Cherry and Plum
White or pink flowers in spring; red or yellow foliage and red or yellow fruits in autumn.

Great care should be taken when choosing a Prunus tree, since there are a few commonly found varieties that are really dull, not to say ugly, for all but two weeks of the year. *Prunus subhirtella* (15 × 15ft/4.5 × 4.5m) varieties are all extremely pretty and elegant – as, for example, P. s. 'Autumnalis Rosea', the Autumn Cherry. Its widely spaced arching and spreading branches form a delicate roundish canopy, decorated from autumn right through unti the following spring with clusters of tiny pale pink flowers.
☐ This is an easy-going group of trees that are not fussy about soil. Although they put up with shade, they will do best in a sunny position.
☐ Train a summer-flowering climber, like Clematis or Honeysuckle, up one of these spring

Small Trees

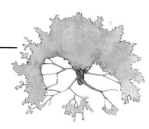

blossom trees to lengthen its flowering season.
☐ See also *Rhus typhina*, Tiered Shrubs, page 149.

PYRUS SALICIFOLIA 'PENDULA'
Willow-leaved Weeping Pear
White flowers in spring; grey foliage in spring and summer

A small silvery green tree
(12 × 10ft / 3.6 × 3m)
with a dense head of weeping
branches and creamy white blossom
in spring.
☐ Ordinary garden soil in sun
or partial shade.
☐ Looks especially good
with purples and yellows;
yellow *Clematis tangutica*
or a large-flowered
deep purple hybrid
Clematis to clamber
through the
foliage.

Pyrus Salicifolia 'Pendula'

SALIX CAPREA 'PENDULA'
Kilmarnock Willow
Silver buds in late winter

A delight in the coldest months of the year, this
small tree (8 × 4ft / 2.4 × 1.2m) has stiffly
pendulous branches, making it look in summer like
a tall bushy mound of mid-green, grey-backed
foliage. In winter, though, it shines with cascades of
grey, furry buds.
☐ Ordinary garden soil in sun or partial shade.
☐ Useful for adding height to a flowerbed without
casting too much shade. Looks especially good with
grey foliage plants.

TAMARIX PENTANDRA Tamarisk
Pink flowers in summer

Sometimes multi-stemmed and shrub-like, this
attractive small tree (12 × 12ft / 3.6 × 3.6m) has a
froth of feathery green foliage tinged with rose-
pink during late summer and early autumn.
☐ Lime-free, well-drained soil and sunny
position. To keep plants bushy, prune in winter.
☐ Looks lovely with plum-coloured
or lime-green foliage; try with
Cotinus coggygria 'Royal purple'
or Hostas.

Large Dramatic-looking Plants

These provide a focal point in a plant arrangement. They may tower over from the back of a border, or take an off-set position – for example, slightly to one side but nearer to the front of a bed. Alternatively, they can stand alone as a magnificent clump. Whatever way you use them, it is best to site them first when planning your scheme; they should be strategically placed to give the best views from your house or garden seating areas.

ANGELICA ARCHANGELICA
Angelica
Green flowers in summer

This tall biennial (6 × 3ft / 1.8 × 1m) has large branching clusters of green flowers in summer.
☐ Moist, rich soil in sun or partial shade. Allow the plants to seed themselves in spring for a repeat display of Angelica flowers each summer.
☐ A lovely plant to add some height and drama to a semi-shaded position. Looks great with Alchemilla at its feet.

CRAMBE CORDIFOLIA
White flowers in summer

A magical plant which makes an enormous mound (6 × 6ft / 1.8 × 1.8m) of large dark green leaves topped by a froth of foamy white flowers in summer.
☐ Rich, well-drained soil in full sun. It takes a few summers before it looks its best.
☐ Perfect for the back of a white flower border, especially with a dark hedge as a backdrop.

CYNARA CARDUNCULUS
Cardoon
Grey leaves; blue flowers in summer

Bold grey-leaved foliage plants (6 × 5ft / 1.8 × 1.5m) with bluish thistle-like flowerheads in summer.
☐ Moist rich soil in full sun.
☐ A great focal point grown on its own or among low-growing grey-leaved plants.

EUPHORBIA CHARACIAS
Spurge
Blue-grey foliage all year; yellow bracts in early summer

An invaluable evergreen shrubby perennial (4 × 4ft / 1.2 × 1.2m) with matt blue-grey foliage arranged in eye-catching spirals. In early summer, large heads of bright sulphur-yellow, flower-like bracts appear at the stem tips.
☐ Ordinary garden soil in sun or partial shade.
☐ Grow with orange or yellow flowers; Nasturtiums or Sweet Peas will clamber through the grey-green foliage in summer.
☐ See also *Fatsia japonica*, Tiered Shrubs, page 149.

FOENICULUM VULGARE Fennel
Green or bronze foliage in summer

A tall clump-forming herb (6 × 3ft / 1.8 × 1m) with finely cut, light green feathery foliage.
F.v. 'Purpureum' is a useful bronze-leaved version. Clusters of pretty cow parsley-like flowers appear in late summer.
☐ Ordinary well-drained garden soil in sunny, sheltered position.
☐ Large clumps of Fennel provide a beautiful foil for a wide range of herbaceous perennials and annual flowers. Try a blue combination with bronze Fennel, Love-in-a-mist, and purple Iris with its bold, sword-like foliage.

GUNNERA MANICATA
Dark green leaves in summer

A magnificent stand of enormous umbrella-sized dark green leaves on tall prickly stems (9ft / 2.7m).
☐ Moist rich soil in light shade and sheltered from strong winds. Cover the crowns of the plants with their dead leaves in winter.
☐ A fabulous waterside feature. Grow with a mass of Ferns and Primulas.

MACLEAYA CORDATA
Plume Poppy
Creamy white flowers in summer

Large, deeply lobed, grey-green leaves with frothy cream-coloured flower plumes throughout the summer. (5 × 3ft / 1.5 × 1m).
☐ Rich soil in sheltered sunny position. Cut down to just above the ground in autumn.
☐ A splendid focal point in a silver or gold border.

MISCANTHUS SINENSIS
Green, grey or variegated foliage in summer

This giant grass makes a splendid clump (5 × 4ft / 1.5 × 1.2m) of upright then arching foliage.
Miscanthus sinensis 'Gracillimus' has greyish green leaves; *M. s.* 'Zebrinus' has leaves with yellow cross-banding.
☐ Ordinary garden soil in sunny position. Cut down the dried grass in late spring to make way for new growth.
☐ Grow with a collection of grasses and Bamboos or use to give some contrast of form in a shrub or herbaceous border.

Large Dramatic-looking Plants

PHORMIUM TENAX
New Zealand Flax
Olive-green or bronze foliage all year

Makes a large dramatic clump (9 × 4ft / 2.7 × 1.2m) of olive-green, upright, spiky leaves. Variegated and purple-bronze varieties are also available.
❑ Rich, moist soil in full sun and sheltered position. Protect from frost with bracken or straw around the base of the plant.
❑ Valuable plant for creating a focal point or providing a contrast of form among shrubs.

RHEUM PALMATUM
Ornamental Rhubarb
Pink or red flowers in summer

Makes a marvellous clump of huge, deeply cut, dark olive-green leaves with tall red or pink plume-like flowers in summer. *R. p.* 'Atrosanguineum' is a purple-leaved variety (5 × 3ft / 1.5 × 1m).
❑ Ordinary garden soil in sunny position, though a rich moist soil will produce better flowers. Cut down flower stems as they fade.
❑ A terrific foliage plant for dramatic effect. Plant in large clumps or among waterside plants.

RODGERSIA
Cream or pink flowers in summer; olive-green leaves in summer

Wonderful bold-leaved perennial with plume-like flowers in summer (4 × 3ft / 1.2 × 1m). *Rodgersia pinnata* has deep green leaves and pink flowers. *R.*

podophylla has handsome heavily veined leaves and cream flowers. *R. aesculifolia* has large horse chestnut-like leaves and pink flowers.
❑ Moist soil in partial shade and sheltered from wind. Cut down flower stems as they fade.
❑ Excellent bog plant for damp areas. Looks best mass-planted or among giant Ferns and Gunnera.

STIPA GIGANTEA Giant Feather Grass
Grey-green leaves in summer and autumn; purple-tinged plumes in summer

A beautiful ornamental grass which forms a large clump of arching leaves (4 × 3ft / 1.2 × 1m).
❑ Ordinary garden soil in full sun.
❑ An isolated clump looks great as a focal point or to provide contrast in a herbaceous or shrub border.

YUCCA
Greyish green or yellow foliage all year; cream flowers in summer

A rosette of pointed leaves (3 × 4ft / 1 × 1.2m) which gradually forms a trunk and branches. Large, cream-coloured, bell-like flowers are carried on mature plants on a tall stem in summer. *Yucca filamentosa* has narrow greyish-green leaves; *Y.f.* 'Variegata' yellow striped leaves; and *Yucca recurvifolia* large rosettes of floppier, narrower leaves.
❑ Ordinary well-drained garden soil in full sun. Cut down faded flowering stem to ground level.
❑ A good visual contrast in a flower or shrub border.

Small Dramatic-looking Plants

*This group of plants is particularly useful for visually breaking up expanses of bushy or carpeting plants. They can, of course, also be used very effectively alone, **en masse**, to provide some really bold ground cover.*

ACANTHUS SPINOSUS
Bear's Breeches
White and purple flowers in summer

A low mound of dark green, thistle-like decidous leaves and, in summer, beautiful spires of white and purple hooded flowers (3–4 × 3ft / 1–1.2 × 1m).
❑ Rich soil in sun or partial shade.

❑ Mix with grey-leaved plants and with other tall spires like Foxgloves, Lupins and Delphiniums.

BERGENIA Elephant's Ears
White or pink flowers in spring

Large, leathery, rounded, evergreen leaves on very short stems make an attractive, spreading clump

Small Dramatic-looking Plants

with spring flowers in shades of pink. *Bergenia cordifolia* 'Purpurea' (8–12 × 12in / 20–30 × 30cm) has a purple tinge to its leaves and dark pink flowers in early spring; *B. stracheyi* has heart-shaped leaves that turn bronze in winter and white spring flowers.
□ Not fussy about soil, thrives in sun or shade.
□ Useful in front border or raised bed.

CROCOSMIA
Montbretia
Red, orange or yellow flowers in mid- to late summer

Tough, fast-growing, deciduous plant that forms large clumps of grass-like foliage with colourful flowers from mid- to late summer. *Crocosmia × crocosmiiflora* 'Bressingham Blaze' (24 × 6in / 60 × 15cm) has red flowers; *C. × c.* 'Solfatare' (24 × 6in / 60 × 15cm) has yellow flowers; and C. masonorum (18 × 6in / 45 × 15cm) has orange flowers, broader pleated foliage and is slower-growing.
□ Well-drained soil in sun or shade. Plant corms in early spring, 4in (10cm) apart and 3in (7.5cm) deep.
□ Grow in drifts beneath trees or large shrubs. Also works well in a container.

DICENTRA SPECTABILIS
Bleeding Heart
White or dark pink and white flowers in early summer

A beautiful plant (3 × 1½ft / 1 × 0.45m) with greyish green, fern-like leaves. In early summer, arching stems carry a neat row of heart-shaped flowers which hang down like earrings.
□ Rich soil in sun or partial shade.
□ Plant towards front of bed or border among ground cover such as Irish Ivy (*Hedera helix* 'Hibernica'); the plant disappears below ground in late summer, so Ivy will fill the gap.

ERYNGIUM Sea Holly
Blue or grey flowers in summer

Thistle-like plant with deeply cut leaves and wonderful steel-blue flowerheads throughout the summer. *Eryngium giganteum* 'Miss Wilmott's Ghost' (3 × 2ft / 1 × 0.6m) is a biennial which will seed itself plentifully to form groups of plants with silvery metallic leaves and pale grey flowers. *E. variifolium* (2–2½ × 1ft / 0.6–0.75 × 0.3m) has evergreen foliage with conspicuous white veining

and blue-grey flowers with a white collar.
□ Ordinary well-drained soil in full sun.
□ Looks good with other grey-leaved plants, especially soft furry ones like Lamb's Ears (*Stachys lanata*) and *Senecio* 'Sunshine', or among clumps of Lavender.

FERNS
Green fronds in spring and summer or all year

Ferns come in many different forms. The great majority fall into one of two groups: those with finely cut fronds like bracken; and those with whole, undivided fronds rather like the popular houseplant, Bird's Nest Fern. *Asplenium scolopendrium*, Hart's Tongue Fern, (1½–2 × 1ft / 0.45–0.60 × 0.30m) has undivided evergreen strap-shaped fronds with slightly wavy edges. *Athyrium filix-femina*, Lady Fern, (1½–3 × 2ft / 0.45–1 × 0.60m), is one of the bracken-like group, with delicate, feathery, lime-green fronds.
□ Shaded position is preferable. Plant in damp weather in spring, and make sure soil never dries out.
□ Plant with woodland or bog plants like Blucbells, Arum Lilies and large-leaved *Rodgersia*. Looks attractive in crevices in damp shady walls, though these conditions mean plant will remain small.

HEMEROCALLIS Day Lily
Pink, purple, maroon, red, orange or yellow flowers in summer

An invaluable plant that forms a bold, eye-catching

Hosta Fortunei

Small Dramatic-looking Plants

clump (2–3 × 2ft / 0.6-1 × 0.6m) of arching, strap-shaped deciduous leaves. In summer, large lily-like flowers appear above the foliage; some are lightly scented.
☐ Any reasonable garden soil in full sun or partial shade.
☐ Looks great with almost everything – from bold-leaved Hostas to bushy shrubs or tall herbaceous perennials.

HOSTA Plantain Lily
Green, grey or variegated foliage from spring to autumn

A plant no garden should be without. Grown for its handsome leaves which form a bold, orderly mound of plain or variegated foliage. Pale lilac flowers appear above the leaves in mid-summer. *Hosta crispula* (1½ × 1½ft / 0.45 × 0.45m) has dark green leaves, broadly edged in white. *H. × tardiana* 'Halcyon' (12 × 12in / 30 × 30cm) has delicate dark blue-green leaves. *H. fortuneii* 'Albopicta' (1½–2 × 1½2ft / 0.45–0.6 × 0.45m) has cream-coloured leaves edged in green. *H. sieboldiana* (2–3 × 2ft / 0.6-1 × 0.6m) is a

magnificent plant with very large, matt, blue-grey leaves.
☐ Well-drained but moist rich soil in sun or shade. Protect young leaves in spring from slug attack.
☐ Plant in a mass under a tree, in clumps near water, or falling elegantly over the edge of a border or raised bed; it also looks good in a pot.

IRIS
Purple, blue, white, cream, yellow, orange, mahogany or multi-coloured flowers in summer

Beautiful flowers and dramatic, sword-shaped leaves make the Bearded Iris a very useful plant. It comes in a wide colour range, from palest ivory to velvety blue-black as well as multi-colours, and new hybrids are being bred all the time. *Iris pallida dalmatica* (3 × 1ft / 1 × 0.3m) has soft purple flowers and fine, bold, blue-grey leaves (variegated varieties are also available). *Iris foetidissima* (1½ × 2ft / 0.45 × 0.6m) is a beardless Iris with glossy dark evergreen leaves; its flowers are insignificant but are followed in autumn by brilliant scarlet berries.
☐ All Irises like sun, although *Iris foetidissima* will put up with quite a lot of shade. The Bearded Iris is not fussy about soil but should be planted only very shallowly. Snip off dead flowerheads as they fade. Trim back leaves of deciduous types in late autumn by making a neat cut across each leaf.
☐ The sword-shaped leaves make a striking contrast when grown among the softer shapes of Gap-Filling Plants (see page 170).

Athyrium Filix-femina

Asplenium Nidus

POLYGONATUM X HYBRIDUM Solomon's Seal
White flowers in early summer

Paired, mid-green, deciduous leaves emerge regularly along arching stems (2½ × 1ft / 75 × 30m).
☐ Ordinary garden soil in sun or light shade. Cut down to ground level in late autumn.
☐ Let the elegant stems arch over clumps of Hostas and Ferns.

Hosta Crispula

Hosta Sieboldiana

Tiered Shrubs

These shrubs are a particular kind of very large dramatic-looking plant. They take up a lot of space, because their branches – or sometimes just their leaves – tend to grow horizontally, giving the plants a somewhat tabular, layered appearance. Use them as you would a large sculpture; standing alone, or at least among less significant plants, so that their form can be fully appreciated.

AILANTHUS ALTISSIMA
Tree of Heaven
Green leaves in summer

When pruned annually to ground level, this fast-growing tree 12 × 8ft (3.6 × 2.4m) forms a clump of vigorous shoots with huge, dramatic, mid-green leaves divided into many leaflets.
☐ Ordinary garden soil in sun or shade.
☐ A tough useful plant for shaded positions. Grow with Ferns and ground cover, such as Hostas.

ARALIA ELATA Japanese Angelica Tree
Cream flowers in late summer

This tall suckering shrub (10 × 6ft / 3 × 1.8m) has huge mid-green leaves divided into many paired leaflets. Foam-like clusters of small creamy flowers are produced in late summer. *Aralia elata*

'Aureovariegata' has yellow-fading-to-cream markings on its leaves, while *A.e.*'Variegata' has creamy white variegations.
☐ Ordinary garden soil in sun or partial shade.
☐ Makes an eye-catching corner feature; grow ground-cover plants beneath it, such as Ivy or mass-planted Astilbes.

CORNUS KOUSA CHINENSIS
Dogwood
White flowers in summer; purple, bronze and red foliage in autumn

In full summer bloom, when the tiered branches are covered in creamy white flower bracts, this large shrub (15 × 10ft / 4.5 × 3m) looks as if someone had poured a giant pot of cream all over it. The foliage turns purple, bronze and red before falling in autumn.

Viburnum

Tiered Shrubs

☐ Ordinary garden soil, preferably lime-free, in full sun.
☐ Grow as an isolated specimen to get the full effect of this magnificent plant.

FATSIA JAPONICA
Green leaves all year

This well-known large leathery-leaved plant makes a dramatic, tiered, sparsely branched shrub or small evergreen tree.
☐ Ordinary garden soil in sun or shade.
☐ A good plant for town gardens, as it will withstand quite a lot of shade, as well as a polluted atmosphere. It provides privacy without taking over the garden. Grow in paving or as a wall shrub with Ivy and Ferns underneath. Also does well in a container.

MAHONIA Oregon Grape
Yellow flowers in winter or spring; dark green leaves all year

Handsome, dark evergreen, yellow-flowering shrub with a tiered foliage form, the leaves being made up of a flatly held, unbranched stem of spiny-edged leaflets. *Mahonia aquifolium* (4 × 5ft / 1.2 × 1.5m) has dark leathery leaflets and rich yellow spring flowers, followed by bluish berries. *M.* × 'Charity' (8 × 8ft / 2.4 × 2.4m) also has dark green leaves but its flowers are carried in winter in long pointed flowerheads. *M.japonica* (8 × 8ft / 2.4 × 2.4m) has dark glossy leaves and loose drooping clusters of yellow scented flowers during late winter and early spring.
☐ Ordinary garden soil in sun or shade. *M.aquifolium* can be grown as ground cover if its main stem tip is pruned back hard after flowering.
☐ A good choice for a shaded place. Brightens up the gloom in winter and early spring, so make sure it can be seen from the house. It also does well in a container. It can be grown as a single bare stem with leaves on the top – rather like a palm tree in shape: just remove the lower branches or leaflets as they appear.

RHUS TYPHINA
Stag's Horn Sumach
Red, yellow and orange leaves in autumn

This tough shrubby tree has attractive large leaves divided into many paired pendulous leaflets and dramatic, angular, widely spaced branches (hence its common name) so that it still looks good in winter when its branches are bare. The leaves reliably turn bright yellow, orange and scarlet in autumn, before falling. *Rhus typhina* 'Laciniata' has deeply cut leaflets that give a lacy effect.
☐ Ordinary garden soil in sun or partial shade. To keep the plant small and shrub-like (4ft / 1.2m or so), prune to the ground every year in early spring. To make a single-stemmed tree, remove suckers and low side branches as they appear.
☐ Underplant with Cotoneaster horizontalis, Autumn Crocus or Cyclamen to create an autumn feature.

SAMBUCUS RACEMOSA 'PLUMOSA AUREA'
Golden Elderberry
White flowers in spring;
red berries in summer;
golden foliage in summer

The golden-leaved variety of this elderberry makes a fast-growing tiered shrub with ragged lime-green foliage. White flowerheads in spring are followed by red berries in summer.
☐ Ordinary garden soil in sun or shade; in a shaded position, the leaves appear to be greener than in the sun. For more foliage and bushier growth at the expense of both flowers and berries, prune to just above ground level each winter.
☐ The bright foliage and strong shape make this shrub very useful for dull shaded positions. Looks great with yellow, orange or purple flowers.

VIBURNUM
White flowers in late spring; red leaves in autumn

One of the most beautiful and useful flowering shrubs, although not all Viburnums have a 'tiered' horizontal branching pattern. *Viburnum plicatum* (8 × 10ft / 2.4 × 3m) is very strongly layered; it has matt, mid-green, heavily ridged leaves that turn dark red in autumn, and white lace-cap hydrangea-type flowers in late spring. The variety *V.p.'Mariesii'* has the most strongly tiered form.
☐ Ordinary moist but well-drained garden soil in sun or partial shade.
☐ A good contrast with rounded bushy shrubs. Also works well in a large pot.

Weeping Shrubs

These are visually somewhat less dramatic than the tiered shrubs, but they do have a very distinctive weeping or, in some cases, arching form. They are particularly useful for screening or shading a sitting area, particularly when space is a little limited – although they are also useful if a contrast of form is needed in a bed or border.

ARUNDINARIA Bamboo
Green foliage all year

Bamboos come in many shapes and sizes – not all of them are Arundinarias but these are the ones most often seen. The Arundinarias are mostly quite tall with mid-green evergreen foliage which billows over the top of attractive canes. *A. mureilae* (7 × 3ft / 2.1 × 1m) forms a large clump of slightly arching stems, while *A. nitida* (9 × 4ft / 2.7 × 1.2m) has purplish canes which are more rigidly upright. *A. variegata* (4 × 6ft / 1.2 × 1.8m) forms dense thickets of dark green canes with variegated foliage.
□ Ordinary or moist garden soil, sheltered from cold winds in sun or partial shade.
□ A stand of Bamboo is attractive as an isolated feature or growing among shrubs and trees, especially beside water. Alternatively, a pathway lined with tall Bamboos make a very attractive and dramatic entrance to a secret garden.

CYTISUS Broom
Yellow, white, pink or red flowers in spring

A group of colourful, stiffly arching, flowering shrubs that produce a vivid cascade of flowers each spring. *Cytisus × praecox,* the Warminster Broom (5 x 5ft / 1.5 × 1.5m) has creamy flowers; the variety *C.x p* 'Allgold' (5 × 5ft / 1.5 × 1.5m) has sulphur-yellow flowers. *Cytisus scoparius,* Common Broom, is a large shrub (8 x 8ft / 2.4 × 2.4m) which makes a huge clump of stiff arching stems, clothed in late spring with white, cream, yellow, pink, orange or red flowers, depending on variety.
□ Ordinary garden soil in full sun. Can be pruned to grow on a single stem.
□ Makes a dramatic focal point. Also good for arching over the edge of steps.

DEUTZIA
White or pink flowers in early summer

A group of beautiful, easy-going, flowering shrubs. *Deutzia × magnifica* (8 × 6ft / 2.4 × 1.8m) and its varieties make lovely white summer flowering bushes with long arching branches. *D. × hybrida* 'Mont Rose' has large rose-pink flowers.
□ Ordinary garden soil in full sun or partial shade. Prune to ground level after flowering.
□ Makes a lovely background for grey and silver foliage plants.

FUCHSIA
Pink, red, orange, purple, white, bi-coloured or single-coloured flowers

This popular little shrub flowers right through the summer, its arching branches festooned with hanging ballerina flowers. One of the best hardy Fuchsias is *Fuchsia magellanica* 'Gracilis Variegata'. It has pointed red and purple flowers and very pretty greyish leaves edged with pink-tinged cream.
□ Well-drained, fertile garden soil in sun or shade. Prune back to the base each autumn.
□ Very useful, shade-tolerant shrub. Works equally well in a shrub border or as a low hedge. Can also be grown in pots and hanging baskets.

GENISTA AETNENSIS
Mount Etna Broom
Yellow flowers in summer

A fabulous sight when in full flower, this magnificent shrub (15 × 15ft / 4.5 × 4.5m) has clouds of golden flowers on its arching stems.
□ Ordinary well-drained soil in full sun.
□ Underplant with low-growing bushes like Hypericum or Potentilla.

PHILADELPHUS Mock Orange
White flowers in summer

This lovely big shrub is a fabulous sight in early summer, when its weeping and arching branches are smothered in pure white flowers scented like orange blossom. *Philadelphus coranarius* 'Aurea' (6 x 6ft / 1.8 × 1.8m) is a golden-leaved form which does best in shade. *P.* 'Belle Etoile' (9 × 7ft / 2.7 × 2.1m) has single flowers, while *P.* 'Virginale' (9 × 8ft / 2.7 × 2.4m) has double ones.
□ Ordinary garden soil in sun or shade.
□ Ideal as a backdrop for a white garden. Also lovely with cottage garden plants like Lilacs and Roses.

ROSA Shrub Roses
Cream, pink, white or red flowers in summer and autumn

At nurseries and garden centres, Roses are usually divided into hybrid teas and floribundas (collectively called bush Roses), and shrub Roses. Among this latter group are many magical arching

Weeping Shrubs

and weeping plants, some beautifully scented and a few that will flower all summer. Shrub Roses don't need the care and attention of bush Roses, which are really grown just for their flowers, although it is often advisable to plant them inside a stout wooden tripod so that their arching branches are well supported. *R.* 'Buff Beauty' (5 × 5ft / 1.5 × 1.5m) is a large-flowered creamy Rose with long arching branches. *R. glauca* is a tall, rather bushy, arching shrub grown less for its pretty little pale pink flowers than for its beautiful matt pink-grey foliage. *R. 'Madamoiselle Hardy'* (5 × 5ft / 1.5 × 1.5m) has pure white flowers. *R. 'Madame Isaac Pereire'* (6 × 6ft / 1.8 × 1.8m) has dark pink flowers in early summer and then again in early autumn. *R. moyesii* 'Geranium' has blood red flowers in early summer followed in autumn by shiny red vase-shaped hips. *R. 'Nevada'* (8 × 8ft / 2.4 × 2.4m) has pale cream flowers with yellow centres throughout the summer. Weeping standard Roses are shrub, climbing or rambling Roses grafted on to a single upright stem. Choose the flower colour you want from the many varieties available.
□ Well-drained ordinary garden soil in full sun.

Provide a strong, well-anchored support or planting frame.
□ Grow shrub Roses among other shrubs or in a Rose garden, and underplant with ground cover like Violas or Pinks. A weeping standard makes a lovely focal point and will grow well in a pot.

SYRINGA VULGARIS Lilac
White, lilac, purple or pink flowers in late spring

Small tree or large shrub (15 × 12ft / 4.5 × 3.6m) with arching branches of grass-green, heart-shaped leaves and beautifully scented late spring flowers in white, lilac, purple or pink.
□ Ordinary garden soil in sun or partial shade. Can be grown as a single-stemmed tree (if side stems are removed) or a large multi-stemmed arching shrub. Dead-head the flowers once they've faded. A branch of lilac can be cut in late autumn and, put in water, will flower indoors a few weeks later.
□ Makes a wonderful arching hedge if plants are spaced 6ft (1.8m) apart. Alternatively, grow with Hosta and Bergenia ground cover.

Large Bushy Shrubs

Along with 'Small Bushy Shrubs', these plants make up the bulk of plants in a garden. Large shrubs often have a magnificence which can earn them a pride of place among other plants – at least for part of the year.

AUCUBA JAPONICA Spotted Laurel
Mid-green or varietaged foliage all year

A handsome, typically Victorian, bushy evergreen shrub with leathery mid-green leaves speckled with yellow. If both male and female shrubs are planted, red berries are carried on the female from autumn until spring. The variety *A. j. 'Salicifolia'* has dramatic, plain green, pointed leaves.
□ Ordinary garden soil in sun or shade.
□ An undemanding evergreen shrub.

BERBERIS Barberry
Yellow flowers in spring; blue or red fruits in autumn; green or purple foliage in summer or all year

This spiny-stemmed shrub makes a rounded bushy

plant with yellow spring flowers, followed by colourful fruits. *Berberis darwinii* (8 × 8ft / 2.4 × 2.4m) has glossy dark evergreen, miniature holly-shaped leaves; it also has masses of rich yellow flowers in late spring, followed by bright blue fruits. *B. thunbergii* (4 × 4ft / 1.2 × 1.2m) is a deciduous plant with pale yellow, late spring flowers speckled with red, followed by small scarlet fruits in autumn; it has spoon-shaped mid-green leaves that turn red in autumn before falling. *B. t. atropurpurea* (4 × 4ft / 1.2 × 1.2m) has maroon- purple leaves which turn red in autumn.
□ Ordinary garden soil in sun (for purple-leaved varieties) or partial shade.
□ Useful easy-going 'filler' shrub. Also makes dense thorny flowering hedge when planted 18in (45cm) apart.

Large Bushy Shrubs

CAMELLIA
White, pink or red flowers in winter or spring; dark leaves all year

---

Very beautiful bushy shrubs (6–12 × 6–12ft / 1.8–3.6 × 1.8–3.6m) with thick, glossy, dark evergreen leaves and gorgeous white or pink, single or double flowers in winter or spring, depending on variety. *Camellia japonica* 'Adolphe Audusson' (8 × 6ft / 2.4 × 1.8m) has scarlet flowers with golden stamens throughout the spring. *C. × williamsii* 'Donation' (8 × 6ft / 2.4 × 3.6m) is also upright but with less full, semi-double silver pink flowers in late winter and early spring.
☐ Rich, well-drained lime-free soil in sun or light shade, sheltered from cold winds. Avoid morning sun in winter or spring.
☐ A great plant for a sophisticated planting scheme. Looks right with glossy-leaved shrubs like *Fatsia japonica,* or Hebes, or with perennials like Lilies. Grow it either free-standing, as a wall shrub or in a container.

CHOISYA TERNATA
Mexican Orange
White flowers in spring; dark green leaves all years

An attractive bushy shrub (6 × 6ft / 1.8 × 1.8m) with leathery dark evergreen leaves divided into neat hand-shaped leaflets. It has clusters of white flowers in late spring and sometimes a few more in summer and autumn.
☐ Ordinary garden soil in sun or partial shade, sheltered from strong winds.
☐ A very useful 'filler' shrub for flopping over the front edge of a border. Mix with other interesting leaf forms like *Euphorbia robbiae* and *Santolina incana.*

CORNUS ALBA
Dogwood
Scarlet stems in winter; variegated foliage in summer

A fast-growing bushy shrub which makes a marvellous clump of dramatic scarlet stems (6 × 4ft / 1.8 × 1.2m) to cheer the winter gloom. *Cornus alba* 'Spaethii' has pale yellow leaves splashed with green during the summer. Other species and varieties have different bark and leaf colours.
☐ Moist soil in sun or partial shade. Cut all stems to just above ground level each spring.

☐ Grow two or three and interplant with winter Cyclamen or early-flowering Crocus; in summer, tall scarlet flowers such as *Lobelia cardinalis* make a dramatic combination with the light variegated foliage.

COTINUS COGGYGRIA 'ROYAL PURPLE'
Smoke Bush
Greyish flowers in summer; maroon-black leaves turn red or yellow in autumn

---

This rounded bush (8 × 8ft / 2.4 × 2.4m) would be well worth growing for its maroon-black leaves alone; in well-drained soil they turn scarlet or yellow before falling in autumn. Its main attraction, though, is its long-lasting, cloud-like, greyish flowers in summer.
☐ Ordinary garden soil in sunny position. Prune to shape in early spring.
☐ A great background to scarlet, mauve, pink or white flowers – try white Lilies and pink perennials like Echinaceas. Also goes well with grey foliage.

HEBE SALICIFOLIA Veronica
White, pink or lavender flowers in summer; dark green leaves all year

---

A neat rounded shrub (6 × 6ft / 1.8 × 1.8m) with tapering evergreen leaves. In summer, 6in (15cm) flower spikes are produced in white, lavender or pink, depending on variety. White varieties are particularly attractive.
☐ Ordinary well-drained garden soil. Dead-head flowers as they fade.
☐ A good companion to Lavender and white Lilies.

HYDRANGEA
White, blue, pink or purple flowers in summer

Not all Hydrangeas are like the ubiquitous pink or blue pompon-flowered mop-heads. *Hydrangea macrophylla* 'Lanarth White' is a pretty lace-cap variety; it makes a rounded bush (4 × 4ft / 1.2 × 1.2m) with lacy white summer flowers with pink or blue tinged centres. *H. paniculata* (10 × 10ft / 3 × 3m) is a lovely bushy shrub with large white flowerheads that turn slightly pink as they fade. *H. quercifolia* (6 × 4ft / 1.8 × 1.2m) makes a loose bush with attractive large dark green leaves and white summer flower clusters that turn purple with age.

Large Bushy Shrubs

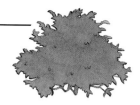

H. villosa (6 × 6ft / 1.8 × 1.8m) is a rounded shrub with matt olive green leaves and large pale purple flowers in summer.
☐ A rich, moist soil gives best results in sun or partial shade, avoiding a position which gets morning sun in the spring. Remove dead flowerheads in spring. Remember that pink varieties will turn bluish on acid soil, and blue ones pinkish on chalky soil.
☐ An excellent container shrub. Alternatively, grow among other shrubs or herbaceous perennials.

MAGNOLIA STELLATA
Star Magnolia
White flowers in spring

One of the smaller, more compact Magnolias, this bushy shrub (8 × 8ft / 2.4 × 2.4m) has icy white, star-shaped flowers covering its bare branches in spring.
☐ Rich, well-drained soil in sun or partial shade, avoiding a position that gets sun on spring mornings.
☐ Best grown in isolation, underplanted with Hellebores.

PAEONIA SUFFRUTICOSA
Tree Paeony
Pink, white or yellow flowers in late spring

This beautiful bushy shrub (6 × 6ft / 1.8 × 1.8m), with its pale olive green leaves, has huge, poppy-like, late spring flowers ranging in colour from white with yellow stamens and dark red markings through to rich yellow and deep pink.
☐ Moist but well-drained, rich soil in sun or partial shade, shaded from early morning spring sunshine. Cut out dead wood.
☐ Plant in isolation with low greyish ground cover, such as *Stachys lanata*. Also makes a lovely wall shrub.

RHODODENDRON
White, cream, pink, scarlet, maroon, purple or lavender flowers in winter, spring or summer

Because there is such an enormous choice among this group of plants, it is a good idea to consult a specialist catalogue or, even better, to visit a specialist nursery during the flowering season. Broadly speaking, plants can be divided into

Rhododendron species; Rhododendron hybrids; deciduous hybrid Azaleas; and evergreen hybrid Azaleas (Azaleas are in fact a type of Rhododendron, not a separate genus). Rhododendron species are a varied group of plants ranging in size from tiny rockery shrubs to huge trees. They may flower any time from mid-winter to late summer, depending on species. Look out for *Rhododendron fulvum* (15 × 10ft / 4.5 × 3m) which has large, dark evergreen leaves with attractive rust-yellow felt on the undersides; flowers are white tinged with pink, and appear in mid-spring. Rhododendron hybrids are the classic large evergreen shrubs with large brightly coloured flowers from mid-spring to early summer. *'Doncaster'* (8 × 8ft / 2.4 × 2.4m) is a beautiful scarlet-flowered hybrid for early summer. Deciduous hybrid Azaleas are usually smaller, with single, trumpet-shaped, sweetly scented flowers. In autumn, their leaves usually change to rich autumnal colours before falling. *'Corneille'* (5 × 4ft / 1.5 × 1.2m) has double creamy flowers flushed deep pink on the outside and very colourful autumn foliage. Evergreen hybrid Azaleas are, on average, smaller than deciduous hybrids and flower in late spring, usually in such profusion that their foliage is completely hidden. This group includes the frost-tender florist's Azaleas, though many hybrids are, in fact, perfectly hardy, such as *'Palestrina'*, an attractive white-flowered hardy hybrid (4 × 3ft / 1.2 x 1m).
☐ Chalk- or lime-free, well-drained soil, preferably in light shade sheltered from strong winds. If your soil is alkaline, you will have to use a container and bought-in acid soil.
☐ Grow under trees – especially Maples and Birches – for a spectacular woodland walk.

ROSMARINUS OFFICINALIS
Rosemary
Grey foliage all year; mauve flowers in spring

No garden should be without this densely spreading shrub (5 × 5ft / 1.5 × 1.5m), which is also so useful in the kitchen. It has very distinctive, dark green, grey-backed foliage which flops very neatly over paving or pot edges, and insignificant pale mauve flowers in spring.
☐ Ordinary well-drained garden soil in sunny position.
☐ Excellent for the front edge of a shrub border, especially with blue-grey and white colour schemes. Also looks good in a large container.

Small Bushy Shrubs

The bushy shrubs usually make up the great bulk of the plants in an arrangement. Their role is to provide a context for other more eye-catching plants – perhaps only stealing the limelight for short periods when they are in full flower, or when all around them looks dismal and lifeless. Small bushy shrubs are especially useful as edging plants or towards the front of an arrangement.

CISTUS Rock Rose
White, pink or purple flowers in early to mid-summer

This sun-loving evergreen comes in all sizes, from 1–8ft (0.3–2.4m). It has large single rose-like flowers with paper thin petals. *Cistus × aguilari* (3 × 5ft/1 × 1.5m) has pure white mid-summer flowers with yellow stamens. *C. crispus* makes a low hummock (2 × 2ft/0.6 × 0.6m) with bright mauve-pink flowers and yellow stamens. *Cistus × purpureus* (3 × 4ft/1 × 1.2m) has dark pink flowers with purple blotches at their centres.
☐ Well-drained, dryish soil in sunny position, protected from cold winds. Trim lightly in spring to keep bushy.
☐ Smaller types do well in rockeries or tumbling over walls. Larger ones mix well with other sunny front-of-the-border-shrubs, such as Santolina or Lavender.

HEBE
Mauve, pink, purple, white or lavender flowers in summer and autumn

A group of neat rounded evergreen shrubs. Some of them are nicely sprawling. *Hebe 'Autumn Glory'* (3 × 3ft/1 × 1m) has dark green leaves with dark lavender flowers during summer and autumn. *H. macracantha* (2 x 2ft/0.6 × 0.6m) has small, neatly arranged olive green leaves and white summer flowers.
☐ Ordinary well-drained garden soil in full sun. Prune straggly stems in spring. Dead-head after flowering.
☐ A very useful 'filler' shrub for the front of a border. Also excellent in a container.

PEROVSKIA ATRIPLICIFOLIA
Russian Sage
Purple flowers in summer; grey foliage in summer; grey stems in winter

A beautiful bushy shrub (3 × 4ft/1 × 1.2m) which looks good in summer and winter. It has dusty grey-green foliage and branching stems of lavender summer flowers. Bare, ghostly, whitish grey stems stand out against the dull browns and evergreens of winter.
☐ Well-drained soil in full sun. Cut the plant right back to ground level each spring.
☐ Plant with red-stemmed Dogwoods (*Cornus*

alba) for some winter drama. In summer, plant purple Violas at its feet to obscure the base of the plant.

PHLOMIS FRUTICOSA
Jerusalem Sage
Yellow flowers in summer; grey leaves all year

A tumbling sprawling bushy shrub (3 × 4ft/1 × 1.2m) with grey, woolly evergreen leaves and curious yellow flowers held in flat round clusters
☐ Rich, well-drained garden soil in full sun. Cut back straggly stems in autumn.
☐ Looks great with other grey-leaved shrubs like Senecio or Santolina. Alternatively, try with *Stachys olympica* ground cover.

POTENTILLA
Yellow, orange or red flowers in summer

Pretty little shrub with a loose bushy shape. Its small dog rose-type flowers are produced right through the summer. *Potentilla arbuscula* (2 × 4ft/0.6 × 1.2m) has soft silver-green leaves and rich yellow summer flowers. *P. fruticosa* has many different-coloured varieties: *'Veichii'* (3 × 3ft/1 × 1m) is pure white with mid-green leaves; *'Red Ace'* (2 × 3ft/0.6 × 1m) has red and orange flowers (on the same plant); *'Vilmoriniana'* (3 × 3ft/1 × 1m) has cream-coloured flowers and fine silvery foliage.
☐ Ordinary well-drained garden soil in full sun. It will tolerate a little shade but tends to flower less well. To keep thick and bushy, remove straggly stems at ground level in spring.
☐ Excellent shrub for the front of a sunny border. Looks marvellous in a rockery or tumbling over a wall.

RUTA GRAVEOLENS 'JACKMAN'S BLUE' Rue
Yellow flowers in mid-summer; blue-green foliage all year

A neat mound (2 × 2ft/0.6 × 0.6m) of distinctly blue-green leaves and yellow flowers in mid summer.
☐ Ordinary well-drained garden soil in sunny position. To keep plants compact, trim in spring.
☐ Not only an excellent leaf colour but also a lovely soft texture. Try with other grey shrubs, such as Senecio and Santolina.

Small Bushy Shrubs

SALVIA OFFICINALIS
Sage
Grey, purple or variegated foliage all year

A really useful and attractive evergreen grey-leaved shrub (2 × 2ft / 0.6 × 0.6m). The small blue summer flowers are best removed as they appear. *'Purpurescens'*, the Purple-leaf Sage, is a very effective foliage plant. Variegated varieties are also available.
☐ Well-drained even sandy soil in full sun. Pinch off flowers to encourage leaf growth. Cut back plants by half each spring.
☐ Grow with other grey-leaved shrubs; looks good with mauve, scarlet or yellow flowers.

SANTOLINA
Cotton Lavender
Bright yellow flowers in summer

A group of pretty, woolly-textured small shrubs. *Santolina chamaecyparissus* makes a neat hummock (2 × 2ft / 0.6 × 0.6m) of grey foliage with bright yellow pompon flowers in summer. *S. virens*

(2 × 2ft / 0.6 × 0.6m) has bright green woolly foliage and the same yellow summer flowers.
☐ Ordinary well-drained soil in full sun. Snip off dead flower stems as they die. Cut back straggly plants by at least half so as to encourage bushy growth.
☐ The beautiful grey or green filigree of foliage makes a good contrast to larger-leaved shrubs. Can also be grown as a low hedge or along a path border.

SENECIO 'SUNSHINE'
Yellow flowers in summer; grey foliage all year

A lovely, grey-leaved, bushy but spreading shrub (3 × 4ft / 1 × 1.2m) with bright yellow daisy flowers in summer. Often called *Senecio greyii*.
☐ Ordinary well-drained garden soil in sun or partial shade. Remove straggly shoots as they appear. Also snip off dead flower stems.
☐ Invaluable at the front of a border. Looks good with other grey-leaved shrubs. Alternatively, contrast its shape and leaf form against an upright cluster of sword-shaped leaves like Iris.

Santolina

Hedging and Topiary Plants

*This is a somewhat different category to all the others, in that it is
a group of plants particularly suited to regular 'man-handling'; from simple
hedge-clipping to intricate shaping into sculptural forms. The mature sizes
of these plants are not really relevant, since these are never attained; instead, a plant's
suitability for use as tall, medium and miniature hedging is given.*

BUXUS SEMPERVIRENS Box
Tiny dark green leaves all year

The only really satisfactory formal miniature
hedge. Very slow-growing, densely branched and
with tiny evergreen leaves – so excellent for cutting
into shapes. Choose the variety *B.s. 'Suffruticosa'* for
miniature edging hedges; and *B.s. 'Pyramidalis;'* for
larger hedges, clipped bushes or other shapes.
□ Ordinary garden soil in sun or partial shade.
Space 9–12in (23–30cm) apart in autumn or spring,
then clip plants to two-thirds their height. Clip
hedges and topiary in late summer.
□ A clipped miniature edging hedge gives a firm
outline shape to a herbaceous bed or border.

FAGUS SYLVATICA Beech
Light or mid-green or maroon foliage in summer;
rust foliage in winter

A marvellous hedge and an especially good choice
for country gardens since it blends wonderfully
well with informal rural hedgerows. The mid-
green leaves turn rust in autumn and remain on the
plant throughout the winter.
□ Ordinary garden soil in sun or partial shade.
Plant 18in (45cm) saplings in autumn and winter,
spaced about 2ft (0.6m) apart. Cut plants back by a
quarter of their height for the first two years, and
thereafter trim once a year in late summer.
□ Reasonably quick to make a good, strong, tall
hedge, but not suitable for topiary.

LAURUS NOBILIS Bay Tree
Dark green foliage all year

Clipped Bay makes a lovely 'architectural' feature,
its dark leaves and bushy slow-growing nature
rendering it the perfect subject for standard round-
headed trees, cones or any simple shapes.
□ Ordinary garden soil in sunny sheltered position.
Clip with secateurs once or twice during the
summer.
□ Best grown in a tub or pot – then it can be moved
to a more sheltered spot in cold windy weather.

LAVANDULA SPICA Lavender
Purple flowers in summer; grey foliage all year

A magical low-growing hedging plant perfect for
lining a cottage garden path, although it can of
course also be used as a small bushy shrub.

□ Ordinary well-drained garden soil in full sun.
Trim off foliage tips and dead flowers in autumn.
□ Best for edging unruly beds of cottage garden
flowers.

PRUNUS LAUROCERASUS
Common Laurel
Mid-green foliage all year

A handsome fast-growing evergreen hedge with
large, glossy, mid-green leaves. Can also be used as
a clipped tree or domed shrub.
□ Ordinary garden soil in sun or shade. Use
secateurs for clipping, and prune as often as
necessary in spring and summer.
□ A good choice for a medium or tall hedge where
quick results are needed in a shaded position.

TAXUS BACCATA Yew
Dark or light green foliage all year

An excellent, slow-growing, traditional plant – in
fact the only truly acceptable conifer hedge. It
makes a solid, many-branched hedge with rich dark
green foliage which can be trimmed to any shape.
Golden foliage varieties are also available.
□ Ordinary, even poor garden soil in sun or shade.
Clip once or twice in summer.
□ Makes a dense, uniform dark green backdrop to
perennial or shrub borders. Best for a medium-
sized hedge and also great for topiary.

TILIA X EUROPAEA Common Lime

Lime has gained a bad reputation because of its use
as a town street tree: aphids living on the young
leaves exude a sticky gunge which drips on to cars
parked below. It has, however, one great virtue in
that it responds excellently to hard pruning. The
French have used this quality to great advantage and
clipped or 'pleached' limes are a common sight in
French town squares. (Pleaching means training –
by pruning – of a row of trees into arches or what is
effectively a hedge on legs.)
□ Ordinary moist but well-drained garden soil in
full sun or partial shade. Clip limes annually in
winter or spring. If aphids become a problem, use a
systemic insecticide.
□ An avenue of pleached limes makes a beautiful
vista. Use a single row of trees either side of a
straight path, or a double row for a wider
driveway.

Wall Shrubs

*These are best described as tall thin shrubs. Unlike climbers,
their stems are usually strong enough to bear their own weight – although
most will appreciate a strong stake or framework to lean on. These shrubs are especially
useful to cover walls around paved areas, where soil space is
limited and yet a climbing plant is not sufficiently full at the base to obscure the ground.*

CEANOTHUS California Lilac
Blue or mauve flowers in spring, summer or
autumn; dark or bright green leaves, often all year

Delightful powder-puff flowers smother this wall
shrub in spring, summer or autumn, depending on
species. *Ceanothus* × 'Autumnal Blue' (10 × 6ft/3
× 1.8m) is a bushy evergreen with dark glossy
leaves and pastel blue flowers from summer until
autumn. *C.* × 'Delight' (10 × 10ft/3 × 3m) is an
evergreen with bright blue spring flowers. *C.*
'Gloire de Versailles' (8 × 8ft/2.4 × 2.4m) is
deciduous, with bright green leaves and large
clusters of sky blue flowers throughout the
summer. *C. thyrsiflorus* (10 × 10ft/3 × 3m) is an
evergreen with light mauve-blue flowers in early
summer. *C. t. repens* (5 × 5ft/1.5 × 1.5m) is a
smaller version and need not be grown against a
wall.
□ Well-drained soil in full sun. Evergreens in
particular need protection from cold winter winds.
Prune overgrown plants in late spring.
□ A great backdrop for a blue border; looks lovely
with Wisteria and Delphiniums. It can be grown as
a free-standing tree in a sheltered position.

CHAENOMELES JAPONICA
Japanese Quince
White, pink, salmon or red flowers in spring

Lovely gnarled deciduous wall shrub (6 × 5ft/1.8
× 1.5m) with beautiful, long-lasting waxy flowers
in spring. *Chaenomeles speciosa* 'Simonsii' has
scarlet flowers; *C.* × *superba* 'Pink Lady' has masses
of mid-pink flowers; and *C.* × *s.* 'Hever Castle' is
salmon pink. Fruits are edible, although these are
not the true edible quince.
□ Ordinary garden soil in sun or shade, though it
will do better in sun. Prune in early summer, after
flowering (unless fruit is wanted).
□ It makes a nice change to have a positive colour
in the garden in spring, and the flowers can last
from very early to very late spring.

COTONEASTER HORIZONTALIS
Pink flowers in late spring; red berries in autumn
and winter

This is one of the most attractive of the
Cotoneasters and is useful as a wall shrub (4 x 6ft/

1.2 × 1.8m). It has frond-like branches which will
splay out flat against both a wall and ground below
so that it grows to fit its position perfectly. Without
a wall, it makes a low ground-cover shrub (2 × 6ft/
0.6 × 1.8m), ideal for covering slopes or waste
ground. Apart from its lovely arching branches, it
has tiny leaves which turn red in autumn before
falling. Small pink flowers appear in late spring.
These are followed by gorgeous scarlet berries
which stay clustered along the branches right
through autumn and winter.
□ Ordinary, even quite poor garden soil,
preferably in sun though partial shade is tolerated.
Prune wrongly placed branches in early spring.
□ Particularly good against white or pink rendered
walls; if they catch the autumn evening sun the
berries will glow beautifully.

HIBISCUS SYRIACUS
White, pink, red, orange, purple, mauve or blue
flowers in summer; dark green foliage in summer

A bushy plant that does best against a wall (6 × 10ft
/1.8 × 3m). It has gorgeous, brightly coloured,
trumpet-shaped flowers and dark green glossy
foliage.
□ Ordinary well-drained soil in full sun, sheltered
from late frosts and early-morning spring
sunshine.
□ Whatever your colour scheme, there is bound to
be a Hibiscus flower colour to match. It looks at its
best among other exotic-looking plants such as
Yuccas or Figs.
□ See also Camellias and Paeonias, Large Bushy
Shrubs, page 152/153.

PYRACANTHA Firethorn
White flowers in spring; orange, yellow or red
berries in autumn; dark green foliage all year

An attractive, easy-going evergreen wall shrub (10
× 6ft/3 × 1.8m) with white spring flowers but,
more magnificently, brilliant autumn berries.
Pyracantha atalantioides has dark evergreen leaves and
large clusters of scarlet berries. *P. a.* 'Aurea' has
yellow berries and *P.* 'Orange Glow' is covered in
tangerine-orange berries well into the winter.
□ Ordinary garden soil in sun or partial shade.
Trim surplus growth between late spring and mid-
summer.
□ A great backdrop for a shrub border. Also very
useful for house walls.

Climbers

*Probably the single most important group
of garden plants; and the smaller your garden, the more
important they are. They can be self-clinging, or they may need
a proper support around which they can wrap their tendrils, such as trellis or wires. Some climbers –
for example, most climbing roses – need their branches to be tied to a support.*

ACTINIDIA
Creamy flowers in summer; pink, white and green leaves in summer

Two useful and attractive species are included in this genus of twining plants. *Actinidia chinensis*, the Kiwi Fruit Vine, (30ft/9m) is fast-growing and has large, dark green leaves and, throughout the summer, creamy flowers that turn to yellow; these are followed by the familiar edible brown hairy fruits. *A. kolomikta* is a smaller, less vigorous plant (12ft/3.6m) but more decorative; in a sheltered, sunny position it produces beautiful leaves that look as if they've been dipped into a pot of white and pink paint.
□ Ordinary lime-free garden soil, preferably rich and well-drained and ideally in sun or partial shade. Both species require some support initially. Prune in late winter to restrict growth.
□ *A. kolomikta* makes a great backdrop to a scarlet planting scheme and looks lovely against red brick.

CAMPSIS RADICANS Trumpet Vine
Red flowers in late summer

This upright, fast-growing climber (40ft/12m) has hanging scarlet trumpet flowers in late summer and, like Ivy, needs no assistance to climb up a house wall or fence since its aerial roots cling like suckers to any surface.
□ Ordinary, well-drained garden soil in a sheltered position in full sun. Prune hard in late winter.
□ A rarely grown but lovely climber – particularly useful for its self-clinging nature. Grow evergreen shrubs in front of it as it becomes bare at the base.

CLEMATIS
White, pink, mauve, purple, yellow or red flowers in spring, summer or autumn; silvery seedheads in autumn

There are enough of these lovely climbers to have them flowering in your garden all year round. For the best range choose from a specialist catalogue. *Clematis alpina* (10ft/3m) has mauve or white lantern-like flowers in late spring. *C. armandii* (30ft/9m) has dark, evergreen leaves (most are deciduous) and large white flowers in spring. *C. macropetala* (15ft/4.5m) has blue or pink bell-shaped nodding flowers in spring, *C. montana* (40ft/12m) is understandably popular since it is so reliable and flowers prolifically; it has small white, pale pink or mauve flowers in late spring or early summer. *C. tangutica*, the orange-peel Clematis (15ft/4.5m) has yellow lantern flowers in late summer and autumn followed by grey silky seed heads. In addition to many species, there are also lots of hybrids to choose from, many with several flowerings late into autumn. Apart from favourites like *C.* × 'Jackmanii Superba' (15ft/4.5m), with its deep velvet purple summer flowers, there are many less obvious and just as beautiful; *C.* × 'Ernest Markham' (15ft/4.5m), for example, has large scarlet flowers throughout the summer.
□ Ordinary, preferably slightly alkaline soil in full sun. Make sure their roots are shaded from direct sun by other plants, or by a tile or slate. Provide a trellis or some wire for it to cling to. Check on pruning requirements for your particular species.
□ One of the best uses for Clematis is to train them up through the branches of other plants.

FREMONTIA CALIFORNICA
Yellow flowers in summer

The downy leaves of this upright climber (15ft/4.5m) are greyish green and many remain on the plant in mild winters. Bright yellow, cup-shaped flowers are produced throughout the summer.
□ Well-drained sandy soil in full sun and sheltered from cold winds. Prune away frosted stems in spring.
□ A lovely cheerful climber for a sunny house wall.

HEDERA Ivy
Plain or variegated leaves all year

The universal climber: handsome, evergreen and needing no support, it has numerous varieties of different shapes and leaf colourings. *Hedera canariensis* 'Variegata' (15ft/4.5m) is a large-leaved ivy with cream and greyish green markings edging a rich green background. *H. colchica* (25ft/7.5m) and its varieties are fast-growing and the dark green, *H. c.* 'Dentata' is a wonderful large-leaved dark green Ivy – also available with creamy edging. *H. helix* (75ft/22.5m) and its many varieties are the most hardy of all and some of the prettiest. *H. h.* 'Goldheart' is a well-known form, with leaves splashed in the centre with cream. The young growth is particularly attractive as it clings tightly and neatly up tall, even quite shaded walls. Many Ivies make marvellous ground-cover plants: *H. h.* 'Hibernica'; for example, is one of the most

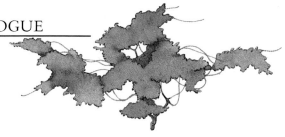

Climbers

effective and has large, plain dark green leaves.
☐ Ordinary garden soil in sun or shade, though most variegated forms do best in sun. Cut back if necessary in early spring.
☐ Ivy makes a marvellous evergreen backdrop for any group of plants, and you can cheer it up by training flowering climbers up through its creeping stems. One magical combination is Ivy with perennial scarlet-flowered Nasturtium (*Tropaeolum speciosum*). Ivy also grows well in a container or as ground cover.

HYDRANGEA PETIOLARIS
Climbing Hydrangea
White flowers in summer

This magnificent white-flowering climber (60ft/18m) will cling on to walls with no help from wires or trellis. Its flowers are held in large frothy heads in mid-summer.
☐ Ordinary, preferably, rich moist garden soil in sun or shade. Prune to shape in spring.
☐ A tall house wall covered from basement to eaves with this plant is an amazing sight in mid-summer. Extend the season by growing other flowering climbers up through the branches. A very useful plant for a gloomy wall or fence.

JASMINUM Jasmine
Yellow flowers in winter or white flowers in summer

Two climbing Jasmine species make very valuable garden plants. *Jasminum nudiflorum*, or Winter Flowering Jasmine, (10ft/3m) will cheer the coldest days of the year, from autumn until spring, with its small bright yellow flowers carried on bare branches; it must be tied to its support. *J. officinale* (30ft/9m), or White Jasmine, has thousands of small, starry, beautifully scented flowers throughout the summer. This bushy climber grows quickly and will twine itself around any support that you provide.
☐ Ordinary well-drained garden soil in sun or partial shade, though Winter Jasmine needs protection from cold winter winds or quick thawing in early-morning winter sun.
☐ Grow Winter Jasmine in a spot where it will be most appreciated – by your front door, for example, with pots of early Narcissus. White Jasmine is best grown close to a sitting area – a perfect plant for scrambling over an arbour.

LONICERA Honeysuckle
Yellow and white or yellow pink and white flowers in summer

There are many beautiful species and varieties of this marvellous plant. A very valuable one is the Japanese Honeysuckle, *Lonicera japonica* 'Halliana' (20ft/6m). It has lovely scented cream and white spidery flowers throughout the summer and autumn, and bright mid-green leaves are evergreen in mild winters. *L. periclymenum* (20ft/6m) is the traditional Honeysuckle of cottage gardens. Its spidery multi-coloured flowers, are dark pink, pastel orange and white.
☐ Ordinary garden soil, in sun or partial shade. Protect the base of the stem from hot sun by shading with another plant or a tile. Prune overgrown plants after flowering.
☐ One of the best cottage garden climbers. Use as a backdrop to a yellow and white scheme or to cover walls in a sitting area where the scent will be appreciated.

PARTHENOCISSUS Virginia Creeper
Green leaves in summer; red leaves in autumn

Crisp green foliage in summer is followed by glorious rich reds in autumn. *Parthenocissus quinquefolia* is the true Virginia Creeper, but *P. tricuspidata*, the Boston Ivy, is more commonly seen.
☐ Ordinary garden soil, preferably rich and moist, in sun or shade. Once they've started to cling they need no further support. Remove unwanted growth in summer.
☐ An easy-going wall-cover plant that looks good against any wall.

PASSIFLORA CAERULEA 'CONSTANCE ELLIOT'
Passion Flower Purple, white and lime-green flowers in summer

Exotic-looking flowers are produced throughout the summer by this prolific climber (20ft/16m); they are basically white, tinged with lime-green and purple. In warm sheltered areas, the flowers are followed in autumn by yellow edible passion fruits.
☐ Ordinary well-drained garden soil in sunny, sheltered position. Prune in spring to restrict size.
☐ The beautiful flowers need to be seen at close quarters to appreciate them fully, so grow them near a seat, in a paved area or over an archway.

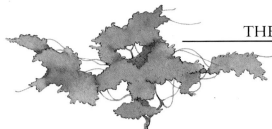

Climbers

ROSA Climbing Rose
Pink, red, yellow, orange or white flowers in summer or autumn

Quite the best of all the climbers, ranging from the heavenly scented ones that flower very briefly to those that flower continuously from early summer to early winter. A specialist nursery is well worth a visit. Some well-known and widely available names to look out for if you get no further than your local garden centre are: *Rosa* 'Albertine', (15ft/4.5m), with double, gorgeously scented coppery pink flowers; *R.* 'Danse du Feu', (12ft/3.6m), with profoundly scarlet double flowers until autumn; *R.* 'Golden Showers' (12ft/3.6m), tough as old boots and with lovely yellow flowers that can go on appearing in early winter; *R. filipes* 'Kiftsgate', a huge plant (50ft/15m) with large trusses of white single fragrant flowers in early summer; *R.* 'Mermaid', another large climber (25ft/7.5m), with enormous yellow flowers in mid-summer, that does well in shade; *R.* 'Mme Gregoire Staechelin' (15ft/4.5m), which has masses of dark orange-pink double flowers in mid-summer; *R.* 'New Dawn' (10ft/3m), which has mouthwatering pale pink flowers throughout the summer; and *R.* 'Zephirine Drouhin' (10ft/3m), a thornless climber which produces bright pink, beautifully scented flowers – often until late autumn.
☐ Ordinary garden soil in a sunny position. Provide them with a support and tie the branches to it regularly. Dead-head after flowering. Most climbing Roses need no pruning; rambling Roses need their flowered stems cutting right back in autumn.
☐ Grow climbing Roses up walls, pillars or over archways; pair one up with a matching or contrasting Clematis for a marvellous display in summer.

TROPAEOLUM Nasturtium
Yellow, orange or scarlet flowers in summer

This group of annual and perennial climbers has vivid orange, yellow or scarlet flowers and fresh green foliage. *Tropaeolum majus* (8ft/2.4m), the annual Nasturtium, is a lovely round-leaved plant that looks great climbing up through other plants – and its bright orange or yellow flowers are an added bonus. *T. speciosum* (15ft/4.5m), the Flame Creeper, is a perennial so it dies right back to the ground each year; it has round leaves divided into pretty oval leaflets and bright scarlet flowers.
☐ Ordinary well-drained soil in sun or partial shade. *T. speciosum* dislikes a chalky soil and needs to have its roots in the shade.
☐ Both perennial and annual species are excellent for brightening up earlier-flowering plants. *T. speciosum* also looks great climbing through foliage plants such as Yew hedges, Holly bushes or a wall of Ivy.

VITIS Grape Vine
Red and orange leaves in autumn; green or purple fruits in autumn

A good choice of large-leaved climber. *Vitis coignetiae* (75ft/22.5m), the Japanese Crimson Glory Vine, for example, is fast-growing with large crinkled leaves that turn brilliant colours in autumn. *V. vinifera* is the true wine grape, and several of its varieties are very attractive. *V. v.* 'Brandt' has purple-black grapes in autumn set among bright green leaves streaked with scarlet. The gorgeous *V. v.* 'Purpurea' has fabulous almost black foliage right through the growing season.
☐ Moist but well-drained rich soil in full sun. Annual winter pruning is necessary to obtain good, edible fruit.
☐ For the Greek taverna look, grow a Grape Vine over a sheltered pergola.

WISTERIA
Lilac or white flowers in late spring

One of the most beautiful climbers there is, with cascades of lilac or white flowers hanging from bare branches in late spring. The fresh lime-green foliage is also very attractive. Various species and varieties are available. *Wisteria floribunda* 'Macobotrys' (30ft/9m) has the longest trailing branches of lilac blue flowers. *W. f.* 'Alba' has lovely white flowers. *W. sinensis*, the Chinese Wisteria, eventually makes a lovely old gnarled plant of huge dimensions (100ft/30m). It has darker leaves and lovely mauve flowers.
☐ Ordinary garden soil will do, although a moist rich one gives better results, in sun or partial shade but sheltered from cold winds and early-morning sun. Prune in late winter to restrict growth and encourage flowering in young plants, and then again in summer.
☐ Let *Wisteria sinensis* and *Rosa filipes* 'Kiftsgate' clamber together over a warm wall for a really spectacular sight in late spring and early summer.

Tall Flowering Spires

*Herbaceous perennials come in a bewildering range of
shapes and sizes. To make life easier when planning a flower border or bed,
they are grouped here into two basic forms. This first group are the tall flowering spires,
which have upright flowerheads, though their foliage may be low
and bushy or a tuft of strap-shaped leaves.*

ACONITUM CARMICHAELII
Monkshood
Blue flowers in late summer

An upright clump of attractive mid-green divided leaves overshadowed in late summer by tall flower stems (4ft/1.2m) ranging from pastel through to deep purple-blue, depending on variety.
☐ Moist but well-drained soil, in sun or partial shade. Both the sap and roots of this plant are poisonous.
☐ A lovely late season bonus, reminiscent of the Delphinium. Grow deep-coloured plants with bright orange Kniphofias (Red Hot Pokers).

ALCEA ROSEA Hollyhock
Yellow, pink, red or white, double or single flowers in summer

A magical cottage-garden spire (8 ft/2.4m) that, if allowed to, will seed itself every year. Flowers come in many shades from white through to maroon, including pastel pinks and yellows.
☐ Ordinary garden soil in full sun. Thin out unwanted self-sown seedlings in autumn.
☐ Let a colony establish itself against your house wall or at the back of any cottage garden border. The leaves often become rather tatty, so disguise them with foreground planting of something like Aquilegia.

CAMASSIA LEICHTLINII
Blue, purple or white flowers in early summer

A pretty, early summer-flowering spire (3 ft/1m) in various blues, purples or whites, depending on variety.
☐ Moist soil in sun or partial shade. Plant bulbs in autumn, 9in (23cm) deep. Remove dead flowerheads when they've faded.
☐ Looks lovely growing in clumps with Hostas.

CAMPANULA Bell Flower
Pink, blue or white flowers in summer

Campanula can be low and bushy or a tall flowering spire. Among the latter type is *Campanula lactiflora* 'Prichard's Variety' (4ft/1.2m), which has violet-blue bell-shaped flowers. *C.l.* 'Lodden Anna' has soft pink flowers. *C. persicifolia* (3 ft/1m) has lilac spires of cup-shaped flowers. *C. p.* 'Alba' is a lovely white variety.

☐ Ordinary garden soil, in sun or partial shade. Support flower stems in windy positions with sticks.
☐ Great in a cottage border with shrub Roses, Lilies and perennial Geraniums. Alternatively, with white, blue or pink herbaceous plants and grey-leaved shrubs.

CIMICIFUGA SIMPLEX Bugbane
White flowers in autumn

Wonderful arching wands (4ft/1.2m) of white bottle-brush autumn flowers. *Cimicifuga simplex* 'Elstead Variety' is the best, with pink-tinged buds that open to pinky white flowers.
☐ Moist soil in light shade.
☐ Looks wonderful when mass-planted as ground cover beneath trees.

DELPHINIUM HYBRIDS
Cream, white, pale and dark blue, lilac, mauve, purple or pink flowers in summer

A really marvellous towering spire in every shade of blue, pink, cream and white; it also varies in height (4–8ft/1.2–2.4m), depending on variety. Choose flower colours from a specialist nursery catalogue to be sure to get what you want.
☐ Good rich, well-drained soil in sunny postion, sheltered from strong winds. Use a slug deterrent around the base of the plants in spring and stake plants as they grow. For fewer, larger flowers, reduce the number of shoots produced by one-third by pinching them out from the base of the plant. When they're over remove flower stems at ground level and you may get a second crop.
☐ A magnificent plant that looks good with many different species. Try interspersing with white Lilies, with foamy Gypsophila in front and taller Crambe behind.

DIGITALIS Foxglove
Yellow, white, pink, purple, red or orange flowers in summer

One of the loveliest of the tall flowering spires. *Digitalis grandiflora*, (2ft/0.6m) is unlike the usual foxglove: it lasts well from year to year, it has ordinary creamy yellow flowers, and its basal rosette of leaves is evergreen. *D. purpurea* (4 ft/1.2m) and its many varieties are the most commonly seen. It is best to treat it as a biennial and

Tall Flowering Spires

to raise or buy new plants every year; it will seed itself but the second generation usually reverts to the true species and produces purple flowers, whatever the variety. Varieties come in many sizes (1–5ft / 0.3–1.5m) and colours, including white, pink, purple, red, yellow and orange.
□ Ordinary, preferably moist garden soil in partial shade. Dead-head the main flower spike when it is over and smaller flowers should be produced. Cut down *D. grandiflora* to its base in autumn.
□ Great in a cottage garden with Hollyhocks, Snapdragons, Verbascum and Sweet Peas. A useful shade-loving plant for growing with Ferns and

Hostas. Will also grow in a container, though not t‹ the same height. Keep away from children, as it is poisonous.

EREMURUS ROBUSTUS
Foxtail Lily
Pink, white or yellow flowers in summer

This beautiful plant makes a stunning tall column c pinkish flowers in summer. Many hybrids are also available, in pure white, pink, palest salmon, and pale yellow. Heights range from 5-10ft (1.5–3m) and the flowering season can be from early to mid-summer.
□ Well-drained, rich soil in sunny position, but ideally shaded from early-morning spring sun. Plant the large, spidery crown in sand just below the soil surface in early autumn. Cut down flower stems once they're over.
□ By the time the flowers open, the foliage has usually died back so grow among the foliage of other plants to hide the gap. Early-flowering hybrids look lovely with Bearded Iris, which will flower at the same time. They all go well with soft grey shrubs like Santolina, Phlomis and Senecio.

Delphinium

Kniphofia

Liatris Spicat‹

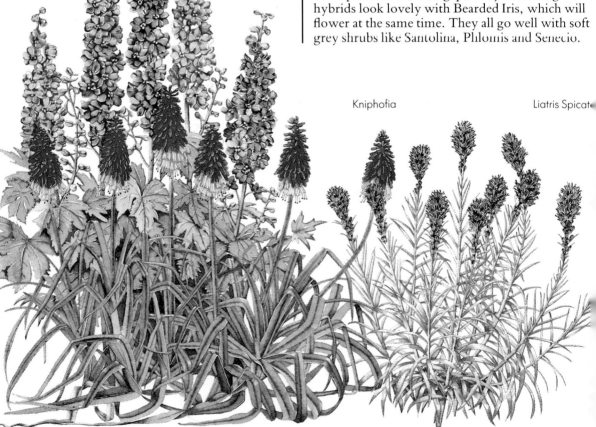

Tall Flowering Spires

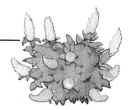

Take care not to overshadow them with very brightly coloured flowers, especially ones of the same shape.

GALTONIA CANDICANS
Summer Hyacinth
White flowers in late summer

A tall spire (4ft / 1.2m) of white pendulous bell-shaped flowers appears in late summer.
☐ Rich, well-drained soil in sunny position. It will seed itself readily but seedlings take four to five years to flower. Plant bulbs in early spring 9in (23cm) deep for flowers later in the same year.
☐ Useful for growing among early-flowering perennials like Delphiniums, as will provide flowers after the earlier species have finished. Will also grow in a container.

KNIPHOFIA
Red Hot Poker
Yellow, orange, red or pink flowers, or combinations of all these, in summer or autumn

This makes a marvellous contrast to many shrubs and other perennials; its unique conical flowerhead, in yellow, orange, scarlet or any combination thereof, always stands out in a crowd. Its size (1–5ft/0.3–1.5m), season and flower shape depend on the hybrid. It makes an attractive clump of grass-like leaves. *Kniphofia caulescens* (4ft / 1.2m) is well worth looking out for; this has soft salmon-pink summer flowers that fade to lime-green, with grey-green grassy leaves.
☐ Ordinary well-drained garden soil in full sun. Remove faded flowers at ground level to encourage a second flush. Cover the plant with its own leaves in winter to protect the crown from becoming too wet.
☐ Goes with almost anything, including shrubs or other herbaceous perennials. For an exotic touch, try with Euphorbia and Bamboo.

LIATRIS SPICATA
White or mauve flowers in summer

An eye-catching plant (2ft / 0.6m) with grassy leaves and distinctive straight bottle-brush flowers in mauve or white (if you choose the variety *Liatris spicata* 'Alba').

☐ Moist but well-drained soil in full sun. No staking required. Flowers start to bloom from the top of the spike downwards; you can remove them individually as they fade.
☐ Great for a contrasting shape to break up a clump of bushy perennials. Best grown in a clump of at least five or six plants.

LIRIOPE MUSCARI
Mauve or white flowers in late summer and autumn

Ground-covering clumps of attractive evergreen grass-like leaves with small columns (1ft/0.3m) of mauve flowers in late summer.
☐ Ordinary garden soil in sun or partial shade. Cut down flowers when they are over to leave attractive leafy clumps.
☐ Useful front-of-border perennial. Also an excellent gap filler.

LOBELIA CARDINALIS
Cardinal flower
Scarlet flowers in summer

Unlike the well-known blue-flowering bedding plant, this perennial has brilliant scarlet-flowering spires (3ft / 1m) on leafy green stems. Hybrids are available with dark maroon leaves.
☐ Moist, rich soil in full sun. A sheltered position is necessary in frosty areas.
☐ A wonderful, richly coloured match for purple flowers like Monkshood.

LUPINUS POLYPHYLLUS
Lupin
Blue, red, pink, purple, yellow or white, often two-tone flowers in early summer

Just about every colour is available as well as two-tone varieties. Easy to grow and especially lovely in large groups.
☐ Ordinary, even poor garden soil, preferably lime-free, in sun or partial shade. Tall varieties may need staking in windy positions. Cut down flowerheads to ground level once they are over to encourage a second crop.
☐ This beautiful neat spire helps bring some order to an unruly cottage garden border. Its tidy, stylish

Tall Flowering Spires

appearance blends equally well with sophisticated, exotic-looking plants.

MATHIOLA INCANA
Stock
Cream, white, pink, mauve or purple flowers in mid-summer

A beautifullly scented spire available in all shades of pink and purple as well as white and cream and in a range of sizes (9–36in / 23–90cm).
☐ Ordinary garden soil in sun or partial shade. Staking is necessary for taller varieties.
☐ Perfect as annual bedding in a cottage garden border. Scatter night-scented Stock seed (*M bicornis*) to fill out gaps and intensify evening perfume.

MOLUCCELLA LAEVIS
Bells of Ireland
Green flowers in summer

An attracive column of lime-green annual flowers.
☐ Ordinary garden soil in full sun. Do not plant the seedlings outside until all danger of spring frosts is over.
☐ An excellent gap-filler for a perennial border. Makes an excellent contrast with yellow flowers and purple foliage. Also contrasts well with white, blue and silver.

SALVIA
Lavender or purple flowers in summer

If Salvias only mean dull ranks of red bedding plants to you, then you are in for a nice surprise. *Salvia haematodes* (3ft / 1m) has lovely loose sprays of lavender flowers in early summer. *S. horminum* (18in / 45cm) is an annual with white, dark pink or purple leaf-like bracts at the tips of its stems throughout the summer. *S. × superba* (2ft / 0.6m) has upright stems of purple flowers in summer.
☐ Ordinary well-drained garden soil in full sun. *S. haematodes* may need staking in exposed sites. Cut down all plants to ground level in late autumn.
☐ Try growing any Salvia with bronze Fennel behind and Alchemilla in front as a contrast. Alternatively, try *S. haematodes* with Acanthus, and *S. × superba* in front of mauve and purple Lupins. *S. horminum* is a handy gap filler for a herbaceous border.

SOLIDAGO
Golden Rod
Yellow flowers in summer

Very easy-going perennial with feathery plumes of golden yellow flowers at the tips of tall stems. Many hybrids are available in different flower colours and sizes (1–7ft / 0.3–2.1m).
☐ Ordinary garden soil in sun or partial shade. Only very tall types need staking. Cut down stems in autumn.
☐ Tall varieties look great as a backdrop to a gold border; grow shorter varieties in groups in the foreground with daisy-like flowers such as Rudbeckias and Helenium in between.

VERBASCUM
Mullein
Yellow flowers in summer; grey foliage

A tall stately spire of yellow flowers with large soft-grey furry leaves. *Verbascum bombyciferum* (5ft / 1.5m) is a biennial with tall slim flower spikes in bright yellow. *V. olympicum* (6ft / 1.8m) is a perennial with an evergreen basal rosette of grey furry leaves and, in summer, tall branching spires of golden yellow flowers.
☐ Ordinary garden soil in full sun. Tall varieties need staking in windy sites. Don't shade the leaves by planting among tall plants. Cut down faded flower stems to ground level in autumn.
☐ Lovely cottage garden plant in front of yellow Hollyhocks, Foxgloves and Sunflowers, with Snapdragons at its feet. Alternatively, grow with other grey-leaved ground-cover plants like *Stachys olympica*.

ZANTEDESCHIA AETHIOPICA 'CROWBOROUGH' Arum Lily
White flowers in spring or summer

The loveliest, and perhaps the most frost-hardy, of the Arums. Beautifully shaped velvety white spathes surround a yellow central spike (the spadix). It has large glossy, dark green, spear-shaped leaves.
☐ Moist soil in full sun. Protect from heavy frost in winter by applying a mulch to the base of the plant.
☐ A stunning sight when grown in a large group beside water, with Hostas and Ferns.

Round-headed Daisy Flowers

*As distinct from tall flowering spires, these perennials have
a flatter or more horizontal shape of flower arrangement.
They include not only the classic daisy flowers, but also
trumpet shapes and round-headed 'umbel' types.*

ACHILLEA
Yarrow
Yellow flowers in summer

A tall perennial with feathery foliage and flat,
tightly packed flowerheads of miniature daisy
flowers which remain attractive throughout the
summer. *Achillea filipendulina* (4ft/1.2m) is an
outstanding species and has some splendid varieties.
A. f. 'Gold Blaze' (4ft/1.2m) for example, has large
flat golden flowerheads.
❑ Ordinary garden soil in full sun. Cut down in
late autumn.
❑ Provides some useful contrast in shape in the
perennial flower border. Looks particularly lovely
with bronze Fennel.

AGAPANTHUS
Blue African Lily
Blue or white flowers in late summer

A handsome clump (1ft/0.3m) of narrow strap-
shaped leaves towered over in summer by tall stems
carrying round heads of small flowers. The
Headbourne hybrids come in white and many
shades of blue and range in height from 2–4ft/(0.6
1.2m).
❑ Ordinary well-drained but moist garden soil in
full sun. Bear in mind that they tend to lean towards
the sun, so positioning needs care.
❑ Excellent in a tub, where the attractive foliage
can also be admired. Grow white ones with
Nerines, deep blue ones with bright orange
Crocosmias.

ALLIUM GIGANTEUM
Ornamental Onion
Lilac or white flowers in spring or summer

The flowers of the ordinary edible onion are
wonderful, but the ornamental species are better
still. *Allium aflatunense* (3ft/1m) produces large,
round, dark lilac flowerheads in late spring. And *A.
giganteum* (4ft/1.2m) has tight round mauve
flowerheads on thick stems in summer.
❑ Ordinary garden soil in full sun. Plant the bulbs
5in (13cm) deep in early autumn.
❑ Lovely against Acanthus foliage to disguise its
own as it dies back, but simultaneous flowering
would be an unusual bonus.

ANEMONE X HYBRIDA
Japanese Anemone
Pink or white flowers in summer

A delightful, easily grown plant (4ft/1.2m) with
saucer-shaped flowers that bloom from late
summer until mid-autumn. *Anemone × hybrida*
'Honorine Jobert' (4ft/1.2m) is a marvellous pure
white variety. 'Queen Charlotte' is soft pink.
❑ Ordinary garden soil in sun or partial shade.
❑ This plant does have a tendency to take over, but
it is so lovely it would be a shame to stop it! Grow
beneath trees for a woodland feeling.

AQUILEGIA VULGARIS
Granny's Bonnet
Blue and white, dark red and pink, lilac and white,
or yellow and cream flowers in early summer

This beautiful plant (1½ft/0.45m) has intricate
bird-like two-tone flowers, usually in varieties of
mixed colours. It has attractive long-lasting foliage.
❑ Ordinary garden soil in sun or partial shade. It
will seed itself readily, unless you cut down the
flower stems after they have faded.
❑ A useful, bushy, cottage garden plant, flowering
after spring bulbs but before the full flush of
summer perennials. Grow with Forget-me-nots
which will provide a foliage foreground to tall
cottage garden flowers.

ASTER Michaelmas Daisy
Purple, mauve, lilac, pink or white flowers in
summer and autumn

The Michaelmas Daisy is a traditional sight in late-
summer and autumn herbaceous borders. But not
all types are to be recommended, as many varieties
suffer badly from powdery mildew while others
flop over gracelessly in the slightest wind. *Aster
ericoides* (2 × 1ft/0.6 × 0.3m) comes in several
different colours and the more compact ones
require no support; all have tiny star-like flowers
from late summer until mid-autumn. *Aster ×
frikartii* 'Monch' (3 × 1ft/0.9 × 0.3m) is an
excellent plant, which flowers from late summer
until mid-autumn; flowers are lavender with orange
centres.
❑ Ordinary, even poor garden soil in sun or partial
shade.
❑ For the best effect, plant in large groups. Lovely
with Nerines and Autumn Crocus.

Round-headed Daisy Flowers

CHRYSANTHEMUM
White, red, pink or yellow flowers in summer or autumn

A large group or plants, most of which do not make a very satisfactory choice for the garden as its intensive breeding in favour of large flower size has undermined hardiness and disease resistance. Some species and a few hybrids are, however, worth growing. *Chrysanthemum maximum*, the Shasta Daisy, for example, makes a large clump (3ft/1m) of white daisies in summer. *C. parthenium* 'Feverfew', also called *Pyrethrum parthenium* (1½ft/0.45m) has masses of small single or double white daisies that seed themselves readily; dwarf varieties are also available. The Korean hybrids (2ft/0.6m) are autumn- flowering and come in a wide range of colours from deep red through shades of pink and yellow to pure white.
□ Ordinary well-drained, preferably slightly chalky garden soil, in sunny position sheltered from strong winds. Staking is usually required. Cut to ground level in winter.
□ Autumn-flowering types are great for late borders. Feverfew is good for path edging.

CLEOME SPINOSA Spider Flower
Pink flowers in summer

A lovely frost-tender annual (3½ft/1.15m) with a round head of pink-tinged flowers.
□ Moist but well-drained soil in full sun. Plant out seedlings each year after the frosts are over.
□ Lovely towards the back of a cottage garden border.

DIANTHUS Garden Pink
Pink or white flowers in summer; grey foliage all year

A low-growing clump (1 × 1ft/0.3 × 0.3m) of bluish grey foliage and pink or white scented flowers, often with intricate markings. Many varieties are available – the Highland hybrids are a particularly good group to choose from.
□ Well-drained, preferably slightly chalky soil in sunny position. In spring, thin out the number of side shoots of new plants by one-third. Dead-head flowers and feed plants as they fade to encourage more blooms.
□ Compact varieties are lovely for edging flower beds. Looks beautiful too growing beneath shrub

roses, provided it gets plenty of sun. Also does well in a container.

ECHINACEA PURPUREA
Purple Cone Flower
Pink-purple flowers in summer

Subtle daisy flowers in pink-purple (3ft/1m) with drooping outer petals radiating from a prominent velvety reddish-brown central cone.
□ Ordinary well-drained garden soil in full sun. Remove dead flowerheads to encourage new growth. Cut down all stems to ground level in autumn.
□ A really gorgeous plant. Grow in large groups with clear purple and pink flowers, like Campanulas. Also works well with yellow, orange and rusty browns, such as Heleniums and Rudbeckias.

HELENIUM AUTUMNALE
Sneezeweed
Yellow, orange or rust flowers in mid-summer to early autumn.

A reliable, easy-going daisy-flowered perennial, with a wide range of flowering times, sizes (2-4ft/0.6–1.2m) and colours, including yellow, orange and rusty reds, depending on variety. The flowers are very distinctive, with blunt-ended petals pointing downwards and slightly away from a central, velvety and ball-like disc.
□ Ordinary garden soil in sunny position. Support the plant using sticks. Dead-head flowers to encourage a second crop.
□ An invaluable and beautiful flower for the yellow, orange or red border. Dark rusty varieties will also go well with purples, pinks and creams.

INULA MAGNIFICA
Yellow flowers in late summer

Wonderful fine-rayed yellow daisy flowers, growing from a large and splendid leafy plant (6 × 3ft/1.8 × 1m) which needs plenty of space. *Inula royleana* is a smaller version (2 × 2ft/0.6 × 0.6m).
□ Ordinary garden soil in full sun. Dead-head flowers as they fade. No staking necessary.
□ A great match for shrubs, and large enough to make its mark even among large bushes. Lovely against purple or silvery leaves.

Round-headed Daisy Flowers

LAVATERA Mallow
Pink or white flowers in summer

A wonderful group of pink or white summer-flowering plants, including shrubs, perennials and annuals. *Lavatera cachemiriana* (6 × 3ft / 1.8 × 1m) has long branches of clear pink flowers throughout the summer. Its leaves are ivy-shaped and soft greyish green in colour. The hybrid *L.* × 'Rosea' (6ft / 1.8m) is more widely spreading and flowers prolifically from early summer to autumn.
☐ Ordinary, even poor garden soil in sun, ideally sheltered from strong winds. No staking necessary.
☐ An excellent backdrop for a pink and white border. Also suitable for a cottage garden.

LILIUM Lily
White, pink, purple, red, orange or yellow flowers in early to mid- or late summer

This group includes some of the most exquisite flowers you can grow. There are very many different types, but most are summer-flowering bulbs with several trumpet-shaped flowers to a stem. Some species are beautifully scented. The best way to choose Lilies is to visit a specialist nursery in the summer flowering season. Some of the best are: *Lilium candidum*, Madonna Lily (4½ft / 1.35m), which produces a magnificent head of ten or more large, white, trumpet-shaped flowers with bright yellow stamens in early to mid-summer and prefers a slightly alkaline soil in full sun; the *L. martagon* group (5ft / 1.5m), whose white, dark or pale pink, or dark red spotted mid-summer flowers hang downwards and have curled-back petals, sometimes said to resemble a Turkish turban; *L. regale* (5ft / 1.5m), which has beautiful white flowers in mid-summer, flushed with purple on the outside and yellow inside; *L. tigrinum*, Tiger Lily, and its hybrids (5ft / 1.5m), which also have the Turk's-cap flowers but tend to be later-flowering and have lemon, orange, red or purple spotted flowers that enjoy a slightly limey soil.
☐ All lilies prefer a well-drained soil; some like chalky soils, others don't mind and some must have no chalk – so find out if you have an alkaline

Lilium Regale

Round-headed Daisy Flowers

(chalky) soil before you choose. Planting depths differ considerably, so check the planting instructions carefully.

☐ An equally good choice for a sophisticated town garden, an exotic plant 'jungle' or a pretty cottage garden. It looks great mass-planted, among perennials or shrubs, or in a container.

MECONOPSIS
Himalayan Blue Poppy
Blue flowers in early summer

A unique group of stunning plants. Perhaps the most beautiful is *Meconopsis grandis* (4½ft / 1.35m), which has large, bright blue nodding poppy flowers on thick stems emerging from a dense clump of large hairy leaves. *M. × sheldonii* 'Branklyn' has huge, face-sized, blue flowers.

☐ A rich, lime-free soil, moist but quick draining, in partial shade and sheltered from strong winds.

☐ Makes a fabulously eye-catching sight in early summer in a blue border.

MONARDA DIDYMA
Sweet Bergamot
Red, pink or mauve flowers in summer

Butterflies are attracted to this pretty perennial (3ft / lm) with flowers rather like a dishevelled pink mop.

☐ Moist soil in sun or partial shade. Staking rarely necessary. Cut back stems in autumn. Dead-head to encourage more flowers.

☐ Perfect towards the back of a pink or purple herbaceous border. Particularly good with Echinaceas.

NERINE BOWDENII
White or pink flowers in autumn

This sugary pink bulb (2ft / 0.6m) is a delight in the autumn just as everything is beginning to look dreary. It has round heads of loosely held flowers in white and various shades of pink, depending on the variety. Its strap-shaped leaves have usually died back by the time the flowers are produced.

☐ Well-drained soil in full sun. Plant bulbs in spring or late summer so that the tops just protrude through the soil.

☐ Looks particularly lovely grown in clumps among grey-leaved evergreens.

NICOTIANA Tobacco Plant
Red, pink, white, yellow or lime-green flowers from summer until autumn

A favourite, sweetly scented bedding plant, the flowers of which seem to last forever. *Nicotiana alata* varieties (2ft / 0.6m) are the most common, but don't buy them until you can see their flower colour or you may end up with a bad clash. *N. sylvestris* is a magnificent, more unusual plant (5ft / 1.5m) with huge tobacco leaves and large heads of nodding trumpet flowers in late summer.

☐ Ordinary garden soil in sun or partial shade but don't plant out until any danger of frost has gone.

☐ A great gap-filler for the herbaceous or cottage border. The lime-green variety is the best; try it among foliage plants like grasses and Bamboo, and sword-shaped Iris leaves.

PAEONIA Herbaceous Peony
White, pink or red flowers in late spring or early summer

No garden should be without this wonderful bushy perennial. *Paeonia lactiflora* (3ft / 1m) produces lovely huge white flowers with yellow stamens in early summer and handsome dark reddish brown foliage. Many hybrids and varieties have evolved from this and other Paeony species; look out for 'Augustus John' (red-pink), 'Karl Rosenfeld' (dark crimson), 'Kelway's Lovely' (deep pink) and 'Sarah Bernhardt' (pale pink). *P. officinalis* also has many attractive varieties, such as *P. o.* 'China Rose' (2 × 2ft / 0.6 × 0.6m), which has pale salmon pink single flowers with dark yellow stamens.

☐ Rich well-drained soil in full sun or partial shade, if possible avoiding a position that gets early-morning sun. Use a fertiliser and mulch every spring. Taller plants may need staking in windy sites. Dead-head the flowers as they die. Cut down foliage in autumn.

☐ Grow spring bulbs among young red Peony shoots and follow them with summer-flowering bulbs tall enough to grow through the foliage.

PAPAVER Poppy
White, pink, red, maroon, orange, yellow or lilac flowers in early to mid-summer

You could make a fabulous multi-coloured collection of Poppies – their lovely papery flowers

Round-headed Daisy Flowers

varying in colour from white, the palest mauves and pinks, through brilliant scarlet to maroon, orange and yellow. *P. nudicaule*, 'the Iceland Poppy' (2ft/0.6m), comes in pink, apricot, orange, yellow and red, has delicate summer flowers on its wire-like stems, and is best grown with biennials. *P. pilosum* (3ft/1m) is perennial and has clusters of large flowers in red and orange. The perennial *Papaper orientale* or Oriental Poppy (3ft/1m), has large flowers in many lovely colours, including pastels as well as clear vivid tones, in early summer which rise above the sprawling hairy leaves. Varieties of *P. rhoeas*, the Shirley Poppy (1½ft/0.45m), are cheerful annuals, derived from the wild field poppy, which flower from early to mid-summer and come in mixed shades of pink.
□ Ordinary, well-drained garden soil in full sun. Tall perennials may need their flower stems staked. Remove dead flower stems as this prevents self-seeding and, in *P. orientale* varieties, may bring about a second flowering in late summer. Simply sprinkle the seed of annuals over the ground in autumn or spring. Sow biennials in late spring for flowers in a year's time.
□ Grow poppies in clumps scattered among other perennials. Use annuals and biennials to hide gaps towards front of border.

PHLOX
White, pink or purple flowers in summer

There are few more reliable and easy-going perennials than this. *Phlox maculata* (3ft/1m) has pretty balls of mauve or white flowers on tall stems throughout the summer. *P. paniculata* (4ft/1.2m) and its many varieties come in many shades of pink, mauve and purple as well as white, and may be dwarf or tall.
□ Ordinary garden soil in sun or partial shade. Tall plants may need staking. In autumn, cut stems down to just above ground level.
□ Another great border perennial, especially for a pink and white scheme. It also looks good among shrub and climbing Roses.

PRIMULA
White, yellow, orange, pink, red, maroon or purple flowers in early summer

Among this large group of plants are some very attractive perennials known as *Candelabra Primulas*. There are several species and many hybrids and varieties that fall within this category, all with flowers arranged in several tiers up their stems arising from a basal rosette of crinkled, tongue-shaped leaves. *Primula pulverulenta* has some beautiful varieties, such as 'Bartley Strain' which is orange-red. Similar to the candelabra type is *P. sikkimensis* and its close relative, the Himalayan Cowslip; these are smaller plants (2ft/0.6m) with narrower leaves. *P. alpicola luna* has creamy yellow flowers, and *P. alpicola violacea* is a pastel shade of purple.
□ Rich, permanently moist soil in full sun or partial shade. Will seed itself readily unless dead flowerheads are removed.
□ Hostas, Ferns and Primulas are a well-tried, successful waterside grouping.

RUDBECKIA Black-eyed Susan
Yellow flowers in summer and autumn

A delightful and easy-going yellow daisy flower, readily recognised by its black central cone. *Rudbeckia fulgida* 'Goldsturm' (3ft/1m) has large and elegant spidery flowers from mid-summer until autumn.
□ Ordinary well-drained garden soil in full sun. Tall varieties may need staking on exposed sites. Dead-head as flowers fade and cut stems down to ground level in late autumn.
□ Another invaluable plant for the herbaceous border.

SEDUM Stonecrop
Red, yellow, pink, white or purple flowers in late summer and autumn

Many species, hybrids and varieties, all valued for their late summer and autumn colour contribution. These are all fleshy, succulent perennials with dense, flat heads of tiny butterfly-attracting star flowers, the colour and size of which depend on variety. *Sedum* × 'Autumn Joy' (2ft/0.6m), for example, has greyish green foliage and flowers that start out dark pink and then, as summer wears on, turn orange and finally red.
□ Ordinary garden soil in full sun. Leave the attractive dead flowerheads on the plant right through the winter. Cut down in spring as new growth starts.
□ A front-of-border perennial which comes into its own as others die off. Plant autumn-flowering pink Nerines among them for freshness of colour.

Gap Fillers

*An extremely useful and attractive group of plants, whose
job is to fill the gaps between other, usually larger, plants.
They tend to have a spreading, though not invasive nature,
so they will not swamp out your prize Lilies or Hostas. They are taller, bushier
and altogether more significant than the carpeting ground-cover plants.*

ALCHEMILLA MOLLIS
Lady's Mantle
Lime-green flowers in summer

The perfect plant for any garden. A crisp, green,
spreading clump of rounded leaves (12 × 15in/30 ×
48cm) with cloudy sprays of tiny lime-yellow
flowers throughout the summer.
□ Ordinary well-drained garden soil in sun or
partial shade. Trim back flowers to ground level
once they are past their best, or leave to seed
themselves if you want an Alchemilla colony.
□ A delightful foil for many perennials; sets off red,
pink, purple or white flowers equally well.

EPIMEDIUM
Bishop's Hat
Yellow, white or pink flowers in summer

Very pretty foliage plant which forms a cushion of
overlapping heart-shaped leaves. *Epimedium
pinnatum colchicum*(1 × 1ft/0.3 × 0.3m) is
evergreen, with leaves that become tinged with red
in autumn; it has yellow flowers on tall wiry stems
throughout the summer. *E. × rubrum* (1 × 1ft/0.3
× 0.3m) is deciduous; its leaves are red-tinted when
young, lime-green in summer and change back to
red at the onset of cold weather in autumn, before
falling; dark pink flowers are produced in late
spring.
□ Moist but well-drained, rich soil in partial shade.
□ Decorative ground-cover plant. Lovely in a soft
carpet beneath trees or on a shady slope.

GERANIUM
Crane's bill
White, pink, mauve, lilac, purple or blue flowers in
summer

The perennial hardy geranium, not to be confused
with its tender window-box cousin, is both useful
and well-behaved. Many attractive species and a
few hybrids flower throughout the summer in a
wide range of white, pink, mauve and blue flower
colours. The best ones make neat leafy clumps that
spread willingly into any gaps between other plants
without swamping less vigorous species.
Geranium endressi (1 1/2 × 2ft/0.45 × 0.6m) has
bright pink flowers; *G. 'Johnson's Blue'* (1 × 2ft/
0.3 × 0.6m) has lavender blue flowers; *G. ×
magnificum* (1 1/2 × 2ft/0.45 × 0.6m) has deep
violet flowers; *G. psilostemon* (3 × 4ft/1 × 1.2m)

has deep fuchsia-pink flowers; and *G. renardii* (1 ×
1ft/0.3 × 0.3m) has pretty white flowers with
delicate red veins.
□ Ordinary garden soil in sun or shade. Cut back
flower stems as they pass their best to encourage
new growth.
□ Choose the right species to give the right flower
colour for your scheme. Looks attractive in any
situation, but particularly well-shaped for spilling
out at the front of a bed, or for growing among
shrubs with bare straggly stems.

GYPSOPHILA PANICULATA
Baby's Breath
White flowers in late summer

This well-known florist's favourite does a similar
job in the garden: that is, it makes a romantic haze
(4 × 4ft/1.2 × 1.2m) of starry-white flowers in late
summer.
□ Ordinary garden soil, preferably with a little
lime or chalk, in full sun. May need staking.
□ Fills the empty spaces left by spring bulbs and
earlier-flowering perennials.

HELLEBORUS
Hellebore
Green, white, pink or purple flowers in early spring

Invaluable for their handsome evergreen leaves and,
above all, its beautiful flowers in winter and early
spring. *Helleborus corsicus* (2 × 3ft/0.6 × 1m) has
lovely greyish toothed leaves, the nodding cup-
shaped flowers are pale green and are produced
from late winter to early spring. *H. foetidus* makes a
mound (1½ × 1½ft/0.45 × 0.45m) of very
dark evergreen leaves and yellow green flowers
throughout the spring. *H. niger*, the Christmas
Rose (1 × 1½ft/0.3 × 0.45m), has lovely pure
white flowers in late winter or early spring. Several
varieties are available, for example *H. f.* 'Louis
Cobbett', with delicate pink-tinged flowers; and *H.
orientalis*, 'the Lenten Rose'(1½ × 1½ft/0.45 ×
0.45m) which is the toughest of the Hellebores and
flowers in early spring in a range of colours from
white to deep purple.
□ Rich, moist but well-drained soil in shade.
Protect early-flowering species with cloches during
very cold weather.
□ An excellent plant for a woodland situation.

Gap Fillers

Grow in the shade of trees and shrubs among spring bulbs.

HYPERICUM CALYCINUM
Rose of Sharon
Yellow flowers in summer

A reliable evergreen ground-cover plant with bright yellow flowers in summer.
☐ Ordinary garden soil in sun or shade.
☐ Useful for shady conditions and dry soil beneath large trees. A bit too rampant to grow among perennials but fine with large shrubs.

TOLMIEA MENZIESII
Pig-a-back Plant
Green and white flowers in mid-summer; green mottled leaves all year

Lovely fresh evergreen mottled leaves form a dense clump (9 × 15in / 23 × 48cm). Spindly green and white flowers appear in mid-summer.
☐ Rich, well-drained soil in sun or partial shade. Leaves in contact with the soil root themselves readily, the new young plants growing from the leaf surface.
☐ Nice bright ground-cover plant. Looks great with grey shrubs, or yellow and blue perennials.

Ground-cover Plants

Mainly for covering the bare soil and smothering weeds, carpeting plants can often also be used in rockeries, or planted in the gaps between paving stones.

AJUGA REPTANS
Bugle
Blue flowers in spring and summer; variegated leaves all year

Excellent evergreen variegated carpet plant (2 x 12in / 5 × 30cm) with small blue flower spikes in spring and summer. *Ajuga reptans* 'Atro purpurea' has shiny foliage; *A. r.* 'Rainbow' has bronze pink and yellow leaves.
☐ Ordinary moist soil in sun or partial shade.
☐ Useful spreading plant for the front of a border. Looks pretty in gravel.

ANTHEMIS NOBILIS
Chamomile
White flowers in summer; feathery aromatic foliage all year

A delightful carpet plant with compact feathery evergreen foliage that smells aromatic when crushed. *Anthemis nobilis* 'Plena' (6 × 12in / 15 × 30cm) has double daisy flowers. *A. n.* 'Treneague' is a dwarf non-flowering form (2 × 12in / 5 × 30cm) used for a Chamomile lawn.
☐ Well-drained, sandy soil in full sun.
☐ Grow in paving cracks in gravel or stone walls. Taller varieties also make nice path edging.

GEUM
Avens
Red, yellow, orange or pink flowers in early summer

This undemanding plant has pretty, cup-shaped, brightly coloured flowers in early summer. These stand on tall wiry stems well above the rosettes of dark green foliage. Geums produces red, orange or pink flowers, depending on species and variety. *Geum rivale* 'Leonard's Variety' (6in × 12in / 15 × 30cm) has nodding creamy pink flowers.
☐ Ordinary garden soil (*G. rivale* and its varieties prefer a moist soil) in sun or shade.
☐ Good front-of-border plant that needs next to no attention.

HEBE 'PAGEI'
White flowers in early summer; grey foliage all year

A useful-low spreading shrub (6 × 24in / 15 × 60cm) with tiny white flowers and small grey evergreen leaves.
☐ Ordinary well-drained garden soil in full sun. Cut back straggly plants in late spring. Dead-head after flowering.
☐ Great edging plant for a grey border. Also works well spilling out of a garden urn or pedestal.

Ground-cover Plants

HELXINE SOLEIROLII
Baby's Tears
Bright green leaves all year

Gorgeous little creeping plant (1 × 9in / 2.5 × 23cm) with miniature bright green foliage which spreads to form a continuous green carpet.
☐ Moist soil that does not dry out, in shade and sheltered from frost.
☐ Delightful ground cover for shaded rocky watersides. Grow it among rocks and stones with Ferns.

LAMIUM
Mauve, white or yellow flowers in summer; plain or variegated foliage all year

A group of ground-smothering grow-anywhere plants. *Lamium galeobdolon* 'Variegatum' (6 × 12in / 15 × 30cm) has fresh evergreen leaves streaked with white, and yellow flowers in early summer. *L. maculatum* has dark evergreen leaves with a white stripe and mauve flowers in early summer. Pink- or white-flowered varieties are also available, as well as one with pretty golden foliage.
☐ Ordinary, even poor garden soil in sun or shade, although golden-leaved forms need a moist soil. Clip after flowering.
☐ Very useful ground cover beneath trees and shrubs or in very shady places.

LYSIMACHIA NUMMULARIA
Creeping Jenny
Yellow flowers in summer; green or golden leaves all year

Very attractive creeping and trailing plant (1 × 24in / 2.5 × 60cm) with bright yellow flowers in summer. A golden-leaved variety is also available.
☐ Ordinary, preferably moist garden soil in sun or partial shade.
☐ Good for trailing over the edge of a pond or in a container.

MENTHA REQUIENII
Creeping Mint
Purple flowers in summer

Tiny carpeting plant (1 × 12in / 2.5 × 30cm) with small leaves that smell minty when they're crushed.
☐ Ordinary well-drained garden soil in sun or partial shade.

☐ Great for planting in paving cracks or gravel. See also Tropaelean, Climbers, page 160.
See also Hedera helix, Climbers, page 158.

SAXIFRAGA
Saxifrage
White or pink flowers in early and mid-summer; green leaves all year

This low-growing herbaceous plant forms a dense evergreen mound of foliage. Its flowers are held well above the leaves. A mossy saxifrage like *Saxifraga x* 'Eddie Campbell' (6 × 12in / 15 × 30cm) has tightly packed evergreen foliage and single, pale pink flowers. *S. × urbium* 'London Pride' (12 × 9in / 30 × 23cm) has dark evergreen, rounded leaves arranged in rosettes and produces sprays of pink flowers on 9in (23cm) stems in early summer.
☐ Ordinary well-drained soil in light shade. Trim off flowers once they are past their best.
☐ Useful low-maintenance evergreen edging plant. London Pride looks lovely on either side of a cottage garden path.

Mentha Requienii

STACHYS OLYMPICA
Lamb's Ears
Purple flowers in summer; grey foliage all year

Gorgeous, grey woolly, ground-cover plant (6 × 12in / 15 × 30cm) making a carpet of evergreen leaves with spires of small mauve flowers in mid-summer. *Stachys olympica* 'Silver Carpet' is a non-flowering variety.
☐ Well-drained soil in a sunny position. *S. o.* 'Silver Carpet' tolerates a poor soil.
☐ Excellent for the front of a grey or white border, but makes a good contrast with any other colours.

Ground-cover Plants

TIARELLA CORDIFOLIA
Foam Flower
Cream flowers in spring; green leaves all year

Attractive evergreen leaves form a continuous
carpet (6in × 2ft / 15 × 60cm) in spring with
feathery cream flowers rising well above the
foliage.
☐ Ordinary moist but well-drained soil in shaded
position.
☐ Grow this easy-going spreading plant in the
shade beneath trees. Looks lovely with Ferns and
Hostas. Also useful at the front of a shady border.

VINCA MINOR
Lesser Periwinkle
Purple or white flowers in spring and summer;
green or variegated leaves all year

A useful ground-cover plant with many varieties.
All have attractive leathery foliage and quickly form
a dense, leafy carpet (8 × 24in / 20 × 60cm). *Vinca
minor* 'Alba' has white flowers. *V. m..* 'Multiplex'
has red-mauve flowers. *'Argentea variegata'* has
cream variegated leaves.
☐ Ordinary garden soil in shade. If untidy, clip
over in winter to encourage bushy growth.
☐ Useful and good-looking ground cover beneath
trees and shrubs.

Stachys Olympica

Vinca Minor

Helxine Soleiroii

VIOLA
Purple, violet, mauve or two-tone flowers in
spring, summer, autumn or winter

The Viola is an extremely valuable and attractive
ground cover which forms a spreading carpet of
dark foliage. *Viola cornuta* (9 × 12in / 23 × 30cm) is a
cushion-like edging plant with mauve or white
flowers throughout spring and summer. *V.
labradorica* (4 × 12in / 10 × 30cm) has rich, purplish-
green evergreen leaves that will quickly colonize
bare ground to form a continuous carpet; it has pale
purple spring flowers. *V. × wittrockiana* (6 × 9in / 15
× 23cm) – the garden Pansy – comes in all flower
sizes and colours and can flower throughout the
year.
☐ Ordinary, well-drained garden soil in sun or
shade. Snip off flowers as they fade to encourage
more flowers to grow.
☐ Great ground cover beneath Roses or in the
shade of shrubs and trees. Also looks pretty in a
container. Buy Pansies when you can see their
flower colours.

Plant Index

Page numbers in italics refer to illustrations and captions.

PHOTOGRAPHIC ACKNOWLEDGMENTS

Michael Boys Syndication 14/15, 16, 16/17, 22, 22/23, 30 bottom, 31, 34/35, 57, 58, 59, 62/63, 69, 71 bottom, 72 top, 72 bottom, 73, 77 right, 80, 84 top left, 90/91, 94/95 top, 94 bottom, 95 bottom, 96 top left, 96 bottom, 96/97 top, 100 left, 100 top, 100 bottom, 101, 103 top, 103 bottom, 106 top left, 106 bottom, 107 bottom, 108/109 top, 108/109 bottom, 109, 110/111, 112 top left, 113 bottom, 116/117, 118/119 top, 118 bottom, 119 bottom, 120 top left, 120 bottom, 127 right, 128/129, 130 left, 130/131 top, 130/131 bottom, 131 bottom, 133 bottom, 136/137 top, 136/137 bottom.

The Garden Picture Library 15, 28/29, 30 top, 38, 42/43, 44, 56 left, 84 bottom, 97 bottom, 136 bottom left.

Linda Burgess/Insight 24, 36 top, 36 bottom, 44/45, 46, 52 bottom, 83 top right, 132/133 top, 132 bottom.